Moon Mother, Moon Daughter

Moon Mother, Moon Daughter

Myths and Rituals that Celebrate
a Girl's Coming-of-Age

Janet Lucy and Terri Allison

With a foreword by Jennifer Louden

FAIR WINDS
PRESS
GLOUCESTER, MASSACHUSETTS

First published in the United States of America in 2002 by
Fair Winds Press
33 Commercial Street
Gloucester, MA 01930

The Myth of the Women's Society on page 143 was reprinted
with permission from *Daughters of Copper Woman*, Harbour
Publishing 2002.

10 9 8 7 6 5 4 3 2 1
Printed and bound in Canada
Library of Congress Cataloging-in-Publication data available
ISBN 1-931412-13-8

Cover illustration ©by Helen D'Souza/www.i2iart.com
Cover design by John Hall
Book design by Mary Ann Guillette

Mikaila, who is now sixteen, was the initial spark that ignited our quest to find a new perspective from which to guide our daughters. Emma, thirteen, Austin, twelve, and Sarah, ten, have inspired the continuation of our journey.

◑○◐

Table of Contents

Acknowledgments

We would like to offer our deepest gratitude to our agent, Jane Jordan Browne of Multimedia Product Development, Inc. She believed in the uniqueness of our idea from the moment she was given our proposal by our friend, J Kahn. Undeterred by our forty previous rejection letters, she found the perfect home for our book at Fair Winds Press.

Our book has been in the very capable hands of three wonderful women at Fair Winds Press: our publisher, Holly Schmidt, our editor, Wendy Simard, and our assistant editor, Janelle Randazza. Holly, Wendy, and Janelle clearly understood the essence of our book and graced it with its beautiful title and cover. Michelle Heller, copy editor extraordinaire, gave it a final polish. Their input throughout our collaboration was invaluable and always on the mark.

Moon Mother, Moon Daughter would never have gotten this far if it weren't for the unwavering support of Jennifer Louden, who generously encouraged us, coached us, and cheered us on, from the very beginning all the way to the finish.

There are many girls and women who have enriched our book by sharing their experiences and stories with us. We are grateful to Mikaila and Emma Allison; Austin and Sarah Clark; Patti, Jessie, and McKensey Smart; Jody, Joya Rose, and Jordan Rachel Thomas; Nancy, Christyn, and Alisha Edmundson; Nona Perram; Terrie Lynn Adden; Colleen McCarthy-Evans; Laurie Counihan-Childs; Angelika Mueller Galbraith and Shirley Mueller; Nancy Gruenstein; Millie Roach; Melitta Slaught; Marina Moses; Carol Castanon; Patricia Selbert; Marcia Sacks; Lisa Schardin; LeeAnn Harper; Carolyn Petry; and Lucinda Eileen.

Our book was blessed by many friends and loved ones who offered essential support in so many loving ways. Jody Thomas, Nancy Friedland, Nancy Edmundson, Terrie Adden, and Patti Smart, who patiently read our first drafts, offered insight and wisdom, and mothered us as well as our children. The budding goddesses in the moon groups showed us that we were on the right path with this idea and courageously joined the journey. Many amazing women and mothers in my weekly writing groups joined me on the path of spiritual self-discovery, connecting with the divine feminine and intuitively reauthoring their lives.

Finally, we would like to offer our love and gratitude to Agnes Leeburn, who taught me true mother-daughter connection; to my father Bill, who loved me no matter what; to Michelle, Amy, and Vince, with whom I have always been deeply connected; to Ed and Millie Roach, who offered much love, comfort, and support throughout the writing of this book and beyond; and to our husbands, Ted and Rob, whose love and confidence in our ability to write this book was essential. Will, the next one's for you.

Foreword

Becoming a Woman

While sitting by the edge of a river in New Mexico, at the age of twenty-seven, I became a woman.

I thought I was simply participating in a woman's wilderness adventure—a little canoeing down my first white-water rapids, communing with nature, and taking some time for writing.

What I was really doing, on those cloudless desert days, surrounded by women twelve to twenty-five years older than myself, was discovering, for the first time, the feminine —unrestrained, intuitive, wise, and raw.

I discovered what it means to be a woman by listening to the stories of women older and more scarred than myself. I discovered what it means to be a woman by charting my own thoughts, trying to tie them down on white paper, scoured by sand. I discovered what it means to be a woman when we canoed ten miles across a lake against what felt like a gale-force headwind.

This was my coming-of-age ceremony.

The Longing

"They are very needed."
"I'd like to have one for my daughters."
"How do I do one?"
"It feels so made up to me."

These are the comments I hear from mothers when we talk about our longing for meaningful coming-of-age ceremonies for our children. We gather in small knots at backyard parties to muse about how we can make things different for our daughters. We trade tales of the ceremony Kim had or the way Zahra hennaed her daughter's hands and feet like her Iranian grandmother did for her daughter. We are hungry for any scrap of an idea, any details.

I think about all this as I gaze at my daughter in the mirror, as I watch her tug her eight-year-old hair into a lopsided bun. I gaze at her wide-open face and I wonder—how can I help her cross the threshold into being a woman? How can I help her learn what it means to be a woman? How can I help her claim her power in a way that helps her own her strength without denying her vulnerability? How can I help her take her first steps into being an adult while staying connected to the mother that loves her? And please, before the ripe old age of twenty-seven.

Janet and Terri

I begged Janet and Terri to stick with this book, reminding them through the project's various lurches that I need it, that so many mothers need it. Janet and Terri did it! They created a menu of meaning and delight. They pass on this comforting idea: even through adolescence, you can stay close to your daughter. Hallelujah!

This book has taught me many wondrous new ways to draw my daughter into the world of women, for the coming-of-age need not be wait until a certain age, it can begin earlier. I love the idea of sharing ideas and experiences over time, creating small yearly rituals that we may harvest as part of her coming-of-age ceremony. I am entranced by the many stories gathering here, stories that show me how other families "do" this transition. Mostly, I'm grateful to be given so many choices to feed our explorations of what it means to become and to be a woman.

Call for Community

This book needs community to fully come alive. Yes, we can create and will craft wonderful individual ceremonies for our daughters from these tools, yet a much more powerful tool lies hidden in these pages: the power to change our culture by bringing these ideas into our communities. I call upon each of us to carry this book into our church, our parent-association meetings, to soccer games and backyard barbecues. I call for us to gather in groups with other mothers and plan our ceremonies together, support each other in creating a brand new vision of mothers and daughters: connected, powerful, communicative, independent, and above all, loving themselves and each other.

I look forward to doing just that. Thank you, Terri and Janet, for your insight and wisdom in reclaiming this link.

Jennifer Louden
Bainbridge Island, Washington
May 2002

Introduction

How would it be different if we looked forward to our daughters' first steps into womanhood with the same anticipation and excitement with which we had anticipated their first walking steps? What if there was a whole community of women waiting to receive them into womanhood? What if there was a way for mothers and daughters to walk together?

These are the questions we began to ask ourselves the day that the idea for this book was conceived. We had been meeting every Monday at the beach to write, and this day was exceptional—crisp, clear, and sunny enough to warrant the umbrella we sat beneath at our favorite seaside restaurant. We had known each other and had worked together for years, though our professional interests had recently taken different directions. Terri is a teacher with the Santa Barbara Homebased Partnership and works with eleven- to fourteen-year-old boys and girls. I am a therapist in private practice and specialize in a process I call *Soul Work—Discover and Celebrate Your True Self*. I work primarily with women, many of them mothers. The two of us share a passion for writing

"Conventional femininity cannot be our guide. We are reinventing the feminine. And most of us have barely begun to appreciate the value or the enormity of this task."

Hope Edelman, *Motherless Daughters*

and have a keen interest in each other's lives, both professional and personal.

Before we would buckle down to work on our own individual writing projects, we would always spend a few luxurious minutes catching up on each other's personal lives and especially on those of our children, who were our strongest bond. We had known each other since they were babies and had cared for each other's children like our own. We exchanged stories about our daughters and shared our observations and feelings about their changing bodies and attitudes as they approached adolescence. We talked about what we would like our daughters to know, both spiritually and practically, as they came of age. Most importantly, we wanted to find a way to stay connected to our daughters. That led us to the library and the bookstores. At a time when there seemed to be a plethora of books and information on puberty, periods, girl power, and parenting, we discovered that something vital was missing: a spiritually focused, coming-of-age book for mothers and daughters to use together.

Through this search we discovered a moon-oriented goddess culture that offered us a new perspective about women. With the moon as a guide and a metaphor, and with the goddess as a central figure, we developed a series of coming-of-age workshops that we called Celebrate the Moon. That summer, six months after our initial meeting at the beach, we were ready to experiment with our ideas. Terri's eleven-year-old daughter Mikaila and a group of her friends were our first recruits. The first moon-group series began at 6:30 P.M. in Terri's backyard; the sessions often ended by the light of the moon.

Each meeting began with the reading of a goddess myth that introduced the topic for the evening. Using these ancient stories and myths, Terri offered the girls a new understanding of their bodies and their monthly cycles.

Through the myth of Hera, for example, the girls were able to understand that menstruation is a natural process that even offers positive qualities. At each weekly meeting the girls discussed self-expression, personal power, assertive communication, intuition, their changing bodies, and their moods and emotions. They also explored their relationships with themselves and others.

Each class included an art activity that reinforced that meeting's specific concepts and ideas. During the session based on self-esteem and assertive communication, for example, the girls created anklets and bracelets to remind themselves of the goddess Oya and of their ability to communicate with confidence. One of the participants, Marina, made her ankle bracelet with clear crystal beads to represent "clarity and confidence in unknown situations." She proudly wore the bracelet at her bat mitzvah as a reminder of her sense of self and her own unique nature. Each meeting then ended with a guided meditation and a journal entry.

The girls' mothers were invited to the final meeting and in a closing ceremony each girl presented her mother with a flower. Each flower was chosen to represent who they were becoming and was presented as they recited, "I used to be (self-description), and now I am (self-description)." All of the girls later had coming-of-age ceremonies, some of which are described in Chapter 12.

Moon Mother, Moon Daughter is a result of the enthusiastic response Terri received from the girls in the moon groups and my similar work with groups of women. This book is the product of our search for a new way to guide and stay connected to our daughters.

COMING-OF-AGE TOGETHER

Moon Mother, Moon Daughter is a spiritually focused book for mothers whose daughters are coming of age. Although this book is primarily intended to be used with girls ages ten to thirteen, many of these activities, concepts, and messages can be shared with girls who are older. *Moon Mother, Moon Daughter* strengthens the connection between mothers and daughters at a time when they are in great danger of disconnecting. It revives the ancient wisdom of coming-of-age traditions that are based on community and spirit. *Moon Mother, Moon Daughter* restores the timeless understanding that the coming-of-age process is one that should be honored and celebrated. This book is intended as a source of wisdom, guidance, and support throughout the coming-of-age years.

Moon Mother, Moon Daughter relies on the wisdom of ancient myths and universal stories. Mythology and storytelling are age-old methods of passing along wisdom, sharing experience, and explaining or teaching about life. Each chapter includes myths and stories about women and goddesses. Using the goddess as an archetype, each story introduces that goddess's key qualities and concepts. For example, a discussion of Tara, the Tibetan goddess of inner wisdom, is included in a chapter on intuition called "Moon Light—Awakening Inner Wisdom and Intuition," and Oya, the African goddess of leadership, rounds out another chapter about confident self-expression.

Each of the twelve chapters introduces key coming-of-age concepts, such as the importance of finding a mentor, creating a supportive and loving community, spending time in nature, understanding natural cycles and rhythms, honoring your body's innate wisdom, using and trusting intuition, and being true to yourself. Each chapter also suggests opportunities for self-discovery and activities for greater awareness. For example, we encourage you and your daughter to keep a daily journal that contains a moon log, a dream diary, and your own personal reflections.

The unique format of this book combines ancient wisdom, practical advice, and fun activities designed to lend support to girls as they reach adolescence. We hope that *Moon Mother, Moon Daughter* will inspire you to help your daughter discover and celebrate her true self. With this book, you and your daughter are guided together.

Throughout the book, Terri and I combine our voices and share the stories of our families, our friends, and our daughters, Mikaila, Emma, Austin, and Sarah. Although we are both the narrators, we use one voice. We have become one mother to our four daughters and therefore use the collective "I" to speak about all the girls and women in this book.

1

Moon Wisdom
Living by the Moon

●◐○◑●

On the eve of winter solstice, my friend Patti and I performed a "vision-seeding ritual" with our daughters. "Ritual" is not a frequently used word in our daughters' vocabularies, nor is it an activity that we engage in on a regular basis, so this was going to be a first. We knew the time had come to offer our daughters a new way to express themselves and claim their own "goddess power." We also wanted to create a meaningful holiday celebration that did not revolve around just getting a bunch of stuff on a Christmas list. When we proposed it, our youngest daughters, who are both ten, were curious and enthusiastic; it was our older daughters, who are seventeen and twelve, who were a little skeptical.

We explained that in ancient times, women gathered in December to celebrate the winter solstice, the dark time of the year that is the source of creative dreams and visions. We told them that our ceremony was a celebration of the end of the dark time, the return of the light, and the beginning of a new year. We planned to plant seeds of intention to represent this new year.

"Scientific experts tell mothers that each child should separate to achieve autonomy. This is a lie. This distorted view of good mothering places a mother's feelings at odds with cultural perceptions of what is necessary for the child's growth and well-being. Moreover, this separation leads mothers into an unintentional betrayal of daughters."

Elizabeth Debold, Idelisse Malave, and Marie Wilson, *The Mother Daughter Revolution*

I wanted to design a simple and fun experience that would gently push the girls' comfort zones to perhaps a deeper place without totally freaking them out. Since Christmas time is traditionally about wish lists, I decided to borrow from this theme and begin with one of my favorite writing exercises.

When we were all assembled in my living room with a cozy fire, some familiar holiday music, and an assortment of red and white candles on the mantle, I passed out pencils, pens, and paper and told them that they were going to get to create a new kind of wish list. I invited them to make a list of anything they would love to do, be, or have, even if it seemed unrealistic. "Use your imagination here," I coached them. "Let yourself imagine that anything is possible—the sky's the limit. You might have fewer than ten or more than twenty wishes on your list. And," I reassured them, "you don't have to read your list out loud."

The girls wanted a little more guidance before they were ready to begin. "Can it be for the world or does it have to be just for us? Can it be a feeling?" They were already a giant step ahead of the game.

After about ten minutes of uncharacteristic silence, I asked them each how many wishes they had. Sarah had four, McKensey had six, Austin had eleven, and Jessie had thirteen. Patti and I had eight and nine respectively.

"Okay, here's the hard part," I informed them. "I want you to see if you can identify your three greatest wishes. This won't negate the others, it just offers you a chance to focus on a few that feel most important. And if you want to keep four or five, that's fine, too. This isn't about limiting our possibilities." I could see that they were really concentrating on this part, and taking it quite seriously! After a few more minutes, everyone had selected their most important wishes. "Now, here's the interesting part," I continued.

"I want you to see if you can figure out what the essence of your wish is. For example, let's say you have a wish for a new car. I often wish I had a sporty little convertible. But what I've learned is that it's not necessarily the car I want, though it sure would be fun. It's more about what the car represents for me. For me, the car is about being carefree and free-spirited. But for someone else," I said, giving a knowing look to Jessie and Austin, who I knew both had car and driving fantasies, "it might be something else."

"Yeah, " offered Jessie, "like freedom."

"And independence," added Austin.

"That's it," I agreed, happy and relieved to see that they were engaged in the ritual and understanding it.

"So what does it mean if you want to fly or to meet fairies?" asked Sarah, who is easily and naturally connected to her dreams and imagination.

"Playfulness," suggested Austin.

"And magic," smiled McKensey.

They loved finding the essential meanings behind their words and pretty soon they all had a clear understanding of the deeper desires behind their wishes. This also allowed them to share the essence of their wishes without giving away the specifics on their lists, and to discover that we had some shared wishes and desires, no matter what our age differences. Peacefulness, freedom, and comfort were some of our recurring themes. The girls learned that if they focused on the essence rather than the specific form, their wishes might show up in many unexpected ways. Everyone seemed to like that idea.

Then it was time for the ceremony.

I passed out green-colored cards cut into the shape of seeds, one for each wish, and gave everyone a brown lunch bag that represented the earth. After we had written our wishes on the seeds, I asked them to sit together in a circle.

I lit a candle and placed it in the middle. Then I told them that we would go around the circle and take turns saying our wishes, either quietly to ourselves or out loud to the group, and then we would drop our seeds into our bags. "When you speak your wish out loud and it is witnessed, it is supercharged exponentially," I told them. "So you might want to consider that, but do whatever feels most comfortable for you."

"Now here's the fun part," I continued. "As soon as someone reads their wish and drops it into their bag, we cheer for them! You can say things like 'Yahoo!' or 'Go, girl,' or you can just clap and hoot, whatever you want. This adds a lot of energy and support to the wish."

And so we did it. Amid laughing and cheering and hooting and clapping, we all planted our seeds of intention for the new year.

Before we got up and headed to the kitchen for our celebratory feast, Jessie made one final comment. "The cool thing is that now that we know what everyone is focusing on for the next year, we can support each other's vision."

Spoken like a true goddess. Our vision-seeding ritual was complete.

THE RETURN OF THE GODDESS

Because of current events and the state of the world today, many women are rediscovering the goddess. They are looking for internal rather that external sources of power in their lives. Feminine deities—from the Virgin Mary to Kwan Yin to female shamans—offer us ancient paradigms and new perspectives to guide us in our lives. In this search for new ways to raise and guide our daughters, many women today are reawakening to feminine values and embracing the goddess within. Our goddess consciousness is returning.

Myths, stories, and archeological findings from all over the world reveal a universal moon-goddess culture that began more than thirty-five thousand years ago. Evidence shows the foundation of these goddess cultures to be egalitarian societies based on a respect for the sacredness of all living things and a reverence for the great mysteries in life.

Ancient peoples who lived close to the earth and in harmony with nature recognized the powerful energy that emanated from the moon and governed life on earth. The ever-changing phases of light and darkness created a balance in nature, and people lived in accordance with the moon's cycles and seasons. They observed the correlation between lunar cycles and the monthly menstrual cycles of women, and therefore gave the moon a female identity.

The moon was seen and known as a powerful force and worshipped as a female deity, a goddess. She was given different names in different cultures—Inanna, Hera, and Isis were just a few—and today she remains one of the oldest symbols of the divine feminine. The correlation between the phases of the moon, the seasons of the year, and the life cycles of women as the maiden, the mother, and the crone forms the basis of goddess mythology. For many of us, our own moonlike nature remains a mystery. But whether a luminous orb or faint sliver, this ever-changing and timeless light can offer insight into our true female nature.

Goddess cultures offer new perspectives, both spiritual and practical, with which we can guide our daughters. Using the goddess and the moon as a guide and a metaphor, we can give our daughters a renewed understanding of their power, energy, and potential.

MOTHER–DAUGHTER ACTIVITY
Moon Journals

To begin your journey, start a moon journal with your daughter. Composed together or separately, these journals can include observations of the moon, its cycles, and its relationship to Earth. Record your moods, emotions, and energy level. Notice the connection between your cycle and that of the moon. Pay particular attention to the new and full moons. Your daughter might especially enjoy keeping a moon log by drawing the moon each night as it appears in the sky for a full month.

The Myth of Demeter and Persephone,
The Classic Mother–Daughter Tale

This myth tells the classic story of mother–daughter separation and then reconnection. It also represents a universal understanding of the seasons of the year and offers a reminder of the correlation between annual cycles, life cycles, and the moon's cycles.

◑○◐

Long ago, there was no winter on the earth and the mortals enjoyed a continuous cycle of flowering, fullness, and renewal. The golden-haired goddess Demeter governed the earth, ensuring that her beloved plants and flowers would always have sunshine and that her mortal children would enjoy her wheat fields year-round. Her inseparable companion was her daughter, Persephone, whom she loved more than life itself. Persephone rarely strayed far from her mother's side, except to run ahead into the fields of flowers that always delighted her. One day, as she frolicked through the meadow, she became enchanted with a flower she had never seen before, one that was deep red, the color of blood. She sensed it held a mystery, so she didn't tell anyone about it, not even her mother.

That night when the moon was full, she tossed and turned, unable to sleep. Her thoughts wandered to the mysterious flower she had seen that day, and she imagined that it called her name. Persephone was a curious young maiden who had never known fear. She slipped quietly out of bed, careful not to wake her mother nearby, and ran for the field, where she easily found the red flower illuminated by the moonlight. Her hand reached for the flower as though it was magnetized, but as soon as she picked it from the earth she felt a rumble beneath her feet and the earth opened up below her. Out of the chasm came a golden chariot drawn by four black horses and commanded by a driver who grabbed her and pulled her in.

Demeter awoke abruptly from a deep sleep to the sound of her daughter's distant cries echoing through her heart. She rushed to the meadow that Persephone loved, but could not find her anywhere. She searched for her daughter day and night, never stopping to rest, eat, or sleep. Fourteen days later the full moon had waned to darkness and Demeter was able to seek the wise counsel of Hecate, the goddess of the dark moon. Though Hecate did not know where Persephone was, she suggested that they go to visit Helios, the all-seeing sun god. Helios told Demeter that Zeus, Persephone's father, had given permission to Hades, the ruler of the underworld, to abduct Persephone and take her as his wife. Demeter's grief then turned to anger, and she declared that the earth would cease to flower. So came the first winter.

But Persephone missed her mother terribly and would not surrender herself to Hades, no matter how he lavished her with gifts. She had refused to eat, until he offered her a pomegranate as red and enchanting as the narcissus flower. She ate six of its ruby-red seeds.

Up on the earth, Demeter's anger had turned to rage and she turned her back on everything she loved, wandering inconsolably as the crops perished and the mortals began to starve. When Zeus could watch this no longer, he agreed to return Persephone to Demeter, but only if she had not eaten anything from the underworld. Persephone was unable to conceal the truth, as the pomegranate juice had stained her lips deep red. Because she had eaten the six seeds, it was decided that she must remain in the underworld for six months each year, but could spend the other six on the earth with her mother. Each year, all the earth rejoices in the spring, when Persephone returns to join her mother in the sunshine, but winter always comes again, and at the end of the harvest season Persephone goes back to the underworld.

◑◯◑

Talk with your daughter about holidays and the seasons of the year. Which ones are your favorites? Why? Notice the correlation between these modern holidays and the ancient celebrations of the Wheel of the Year. You might like to get to know the goddesses associated with the holidays we celebrate today. There are many books that offer insight on the roots of our modern holidays.

The myth of Demeter and Persephone is a story about many things—the mother–daughter relationship, the seasons of the year, and the cycle of life. In moon-based mythology and goddess spirituality, the stages of a woman's life are referred to as the maiden, mother, and crone. Demeter and Persephone, along with Hecate, represent the three phases of a woman's life and the three phases of the moon. Persephone, the goddess of springtime, is like the waxing moon, a maiden full of promise and potential. Demeter, known as the goddess of the grain and harvest, is the full moon. As the mother of the earth, she governs the seasons. Hecate, the wise crone, is the goddess of the waning and dark moon. She represents old age and death. This popular myth, which originated in Greece, was used in many ancient cultures and religions to explain the seasons of the year. This cycle of seasons, known as the Wheel of the Year, has been recognized and celebrated for thousands of years.

THE WHEEL OF THE YEAR

The Wheel of the Year, based on the sun and moon, was a series of eight festivals and celebrations that were practiced each year in Europe, specifically by the Greeks, Romans, and Celts. These festivals or holy-day celebrations signaled to the people when to plant, when to harvest, and when to carry out the other important activities of their lives. The Wheel of the Year follows the growing cycle through the seasons and at the same time symbolizes the life cycle, with each holy day marking a new stage of life. Birth is marked by the winter solstice, maidenhood by the spring equinox, motherhood by the summer solstice, and death by Hallows, or Halloween.

The Wheel of the Year includes the following eight holy days, or 'sabbats,' occurring every six weeks: winter solstice (December 20–23), Candlemas (February 2), the spring equinox (March 20–23), Beltane (May 1), summer solstice (June 20–23), Lammas (August 1), the fall equinox (September 20–23), and Hallows (October 31).

THE MOTHER–DAUGHTER RELATIONSHIP

As our own daughters began to come of age, we wondered if this was the beginning of an inevitable separation between mothers and daughters that seemed characteristic of adolescence. But intuitively, mother–daughter separation did not feel right to us. We now believe that mother–daughter separation is neither inevitable nor desirable.

A current of change sweeps over women in their late thirties and forties. It is a time when we carefully reconsider our values and re-evaluate our lives. It is also a time when most women begin to develop a sense of authenticity and start to create outer lives that more closely reflect their inner values. We begin to make our way to this new place by using intuition as our guide. As we cross the threshold into the second half of our lives, women often experience enhanced intuition, creativity, power, and wisdom.

In ancient times, coming-of-age girls sought guidance from the wise women in their communities, but girls today are most often guided by their peers, the media, and a culture that does not honor or support them. It is a time in which girls often disconnect from themselves and start to separate from their mothers. As we begin to create more meaningful and authentic lives for ourselves, we have an opportunity for parallel journeys of growth with our daughters, journeys that would allow us to share our wisdom with them.

Like the moon, the mother–daughter relationship has natural cycles of waxing and waning, but our daughters' coming-of-age experiences offer an opportunity to bring the

On the night of the next full moon, take a "moon walk" with your daughter. Look into the night sky as you walk together. Notice everything around you. What do you see, hear, smell, and feel? Pay attention to the changing seasons. Make these monthly connections with your daughter and the moon a priority.

relationship to a new fullness. Through this book we seek to honor the changing seasons of a mother–daughter relationship and offer a different, more connected coming-of-age.

The Modern-Day Demeter and Persephone

The modern-day Demeter and Persephone have a close and loving relationship. They understand that their own relationship waxes and wanes and has its own natural seasons. Like all cycles of beginnings and endings, they know that their relationship comes full circle, but through it all they stay connected.

2
Moon Light
Awakening Inner Wisdom and Intuition

●◑○◑●

When my friend Melitta died of cancer at age 35, I was filled with grief, confusion, and questions. Our early lives had been shaped by the same painful experiences, and we had been on a shared path for many years, both of us questing for spiritual knowledge and healing. We'd come a long way together, and then she was gone.

At that time, I was a busy working mother with two young daughters, ages one and four. Though I was living an outwardly full life, complete with marriage, career, and motherhood, I had a deep sense that something essential was missing. As full as my life appeared, I felt depleted, exhausted, and empty on the inside. Fueled primarily by caffeine and adrenaline, I was living on a treadmill, running and rushing from one event to the next.

Melitta's death literally stopped me in my tracks. I knew I would need to go inward before I could go onward. The longing that had been silently tugging on my sleeve—begging me to slow down, to get quiet, to be still—now had a quality of urgency. Unable to ignore the call from within, I took a leave of absence from my part-time teaching job and

"Intuition is a spiritual faculty and does not explain but simply points the way."

Florence Scovel Shinn,
The Wisdom of Florence Shinn

called it a sabbatical, which literally means "to rest and to worship." I kept my one-year-old in home day care in the morning while my four-year-old was at preschool, and for the first time in my life, I consciously created solitude.

Spending time alone was not something I was familiar with or all that comfortable with, yet the craving I had for silence and stillness guided my journey. Winter in Santa Barbara is a beautiful time, and the beaches are relatively empty. I took long, leisurely, barefoot walks along the sandy shore, something I have loved to do since I was a girl. I filled my pockets with seashells and beach glass and I carried my journal everywhere I went. My new, unhurried pace seemed to offer me all the time in the universe, and I would often spend hours just sitting and looking out at the ocean. I'm not sure what I was looking for, but I wanted some kind of a sign, something that would show me or tell me the answers to my deepest questions. I will admit, my greatest hope was to see something extraordinary—a giant cross, a luminous angel, the face of God, whatever it was, and I wasn't feeling very picky.

And then one day it happened, but not as I had imagined. While sitting on a bluff overlooking the ocean, I heard a voice, speaking directly and clearly to me. It wasn't a man's deep baritone, or the voice of some foreign entity. It was the faint sound of my own true voice, speaking with a clear and gentle wisdom I had never heard before. The truth I had been searching for outside myself and looking for out on the ocean spoke to me in a still, small voice from within. I had just needed to get quiet and still enough to hear it.

The voice I heard that day was the voice of my intuition, my own inner compass and "way shower." Guided from within, my life at that moment took a whole new direction, and I was ready to go forward.

That was eight years ago. Today, I can honestly say that the voice I first heard on the bluff over the ocean is still alive and well within me. At times it has gotten louder and at other times it has been almost inaudible. Sometimes the voice gets fuzzy with static, and I have had periods of disconnection. But I have found a few ways to reconnect with myself and to stay plugged in.

THE VOICE OF INTUITION

When asked over and over again about her connection to her intuition, Echo Bodine, author of *A Still, Small Voice—A Psychic's Guide to Awakening Intuition* replies, "I was raised by a mother who taught me to live this way. Listening to my inner voice started as far back as I can remember, and there wasn't any formal training. My mother simply said, repeatedly, 'Listen to the voice inside.'"

Unfortunately, I don't believe that Echo's experience was the norm, nor was her mother's guidance what most of us received. Most of us learned to listen to other voices—the voices outside ourselves rather than the voice within.

Teachers, ministers, family members, and friends are the external voices that we internalize and often live by. They drown out our true inner voice and make it hard to hear. It is important to take the time to listen carefully, trust what our inner voice says, and do what feels right.

STAYING PLUGGED IN—CREATING A SPIRITUAL PRACTICE TO HEAR THE VOICE WITHIN

For most of us, the hardest part about creating a spiritual practice is showing up.

My primary spiritual practice is the intuitive and spontaneous journal writing that I do every morning. Showing up each day and writing faithfully has allowed me to stay connected to my inner voice. This daily ritual provides the structure I need to quiet the external voices and reconnect with my internal wisdom. Amazing things have come through my pen and given me a renewed perspective to guide my daily life. I have often been grateful for the truth and clarity this connection provides, which have allowed me to tackle problems and larger issues in my life.

My friend Lynn has kept a journal since she got her first lock-and-key diary at age thirteen. She has written more consistently than anyone I know for almost her entire life, and has kept every one of her journals. In the last few years, she has made some pretty courageous choices and changes in her life based on a commitment to be true to herself. "When I read back over my journals, it was always there, the voice of truth. I just didn't always trust it or know how to follow my own inner wisdom. That is the most important thing that I want to be different for my daughter."

There are many ways of quieting our minds to hear the voice within. My friend Carol wakes up early every morning and meditates. Even when we are camping together, she makes sure to spend at least twenty minutes alone in her tent. It has taken practice and she has had to work hard to remind her family not to interrupt her during her meditation time. If it is hard for you to quiet your mind, a meditation tape, headphones, and a portable tape player can help you get started. The quiet soothing voice guiding your journey inward helps quiet any external voices. A long walk or swim can be meditative as well.

Spiritual practices can be active, creative, or still, and can vary from day to day.

For ideas about spiritual practices, I turned to my friend Jennifer Louden, author of *The Comfort Queen's Guide to Life*. She has a Web site (www.comfortqueen.com) and a monthly newsletter in which she shares her own personal daily practices and invites her readers to do the same.

Here's a sampling from one of her newsletters:

Lisa writes: "I'll take you up on your offer to share my daily practice, because it is something relatively new in my life and I am finding such joy in it. Early in the morning, before my husband and two boys (ages one and three) get up, I dance. I surf the 70's, 80's and hard-rock music stations on our satellite and just "trip the light fantastic." While my endorphins are popping after about forty minutes of dancing, I turn to the New Age station and cool down and stretch and breathe and start to listen to my inner voice. I follow that with a guided meditation tape I created myself, which includes positive affirmations about my life and creative spirit. I've also created a form I use daily to remind me of my ten most important habits (movement, meditation, water, family prayer time, etc.) along with what I'd like to accomplish, both outer and inner, during the day. On the days I don't follow this practice I have found a real lack of focus, so it has become very important to me."

"Daily Practice should be a 'guilt-free zone,'" writes Marcia Sacks, a meditation teacher and writer in the Chicago area. "Guilt is probably one of the most devastating emotions we can bring into this process. You know how it is—you promise to yourself, 'I'm going to meditate every day this year!' Then all of a sudden you miss one day and you're devastated. 'Oh, no—I blew it! I'm a bad person. How could I have done this? I've broken my vow!' Then you realize you've spent so much time being guilty that you didn't meditate the next day, either. Then you think, 'I've blown it forever. I've ruined my next twelve lifetimes!'

Help your daughter consciously create a spiritual practice. Remind her that quieting her mind and relaxing her body are practices that allow her to enhance her inner knowledge and hear her voice within. Notice the natural ways she already stills her body and quiets her mind, and consciously acknowledge what she is already doing. Adding a candle to her evening bath or soothing music to her bedtime ritual can create the right atmosphere and transform a daily routine into a spiritual practice. A guided meditation at bedtime is great as well. Teaching our daughters a few spiritual practices can be the beginning of an intuitive life.

Even when it's not logical, we can begin to think that way. We have to realize that there is not a guy sitting up there on a cloud with a report card going, 'You get an F in meditation. You've blown the semester.' It just doesn't work that way."

CREATING SPIRITUAL PRACTICES FOR OUR DAUGHTERS

Spiritual practices are not just for mothers—they are important for daughters, too. As a matter of fact, your daughter may be more receptive than you think. As mothers, we can set a positive tone for our daughters by making spirituality a part of who we are and how we live. It takes practice and a bit of getting used to, but our experience has shown that young girls hunger for opportunities like this. They are really not that far away from the goddess within, they just need to be reminded of her and guided to her. Start with your daughter's interests. Is it art, writing, nature, music? Plan activities that you know she likes and is already familiar with. And if it doesn't work—try again. Your perseverance will pay off.

Last Saturday, my daughter's eleven-year-old friend Claire came over and we made prayer boxes. They are hand-decorated boxes that are used as a place to put written wishes, prayers, problems, or special requests that require divine assistance and guidance. I rounded up an assortment of left-over boxes—a few small gift boxes and some empty checkbook boxes—and I pulled out the big bag of fabric scraps I keep in the hall closet. I also gathered recycled wrapping paper, beads, and glitter, and I even cut up my old dark-blue velvet skirt to line the inside of the boxes. We shared scissors and passed around a couple of glue sticks and a big bottle of glue. Claire made one for her mom, whose birthday was the next day. "My mom's into prayers and angels, too," she told us as she cut out angels from the wrapping paper and glued them on her box. After we had finished our project and were admiring each other's creations—each as unique as the one who made it—we talked about how to use the box and about the different ways to ask for help and guidance. The prayer box was the start of a spiritual practice for Claire and her mother to share together.

The girls in the moon group learned a spiritual practice they could do at home with their families. After an evening of storytelling and activities, we would gather in my living room, lower the lights, light candles, put on quiet music, and be still. The girls could write or sit quietly. After a couple of sessions that usually began with giggling, this became the favorite part of the meetings and they were soon able to settle in quickly. Ten to fifteen minutes was generally enough, although they often craved more. They loved the quiet time, the soothing music, the candlelight, and the mystical feeling of it all. It was as if they were connected directly to their souls. They did not need to think or do anything, they just were. When it was time to finish, they stretched and came back with reluctance—they didn't want the spell to be broken. With practice, you can create a similar experience at home. Turn off the TV, gather your family around (husbands and sons welcome!), and take ten minutes to be quiet together. And don't give up! There will be many distractions—phone calls, homework, evening commitments—but keep trying and see what happens.

Tibetan Buddhists view life as a process and a journey, one that allows them to achieve inner wisdom and knowledge. They call this inner wisdom and knowledge "enlightenment." They believe that enlightenment leads to inner peace and true happiness, which are more valuable than anything else in the world. Such an enlightened person is called a Buddha, or "blessed one." The people of Tibet worship Buddha as their god and great teacher. Buddha, once a young man of ancient India named Siddhartha, set out on his own life's journey of suffering and hardship (physical and spiritual discipline) and achieved enlightenment. The goddess Tara also sought enlightenment and became the first female Buddha. The teachings of Buddha form the basis of Buddhism, a major Eastern religion. Buddhists seek wisdom, meaning, inner peace, and freedom through daily spiritual practices or "disciplines." Meditation is a Buddhist discipline and spiritual practice used by many people around the world to still the mind and access spiritual guidance and inner knowing. Inner wisdom and knowledge are available to all of us.

The Myth of Tara, the Tibetan Goddess of Inner Wisdom

When the first rays of sunlight peeked over the horizon, the goddess Tara was already in her lotus position, sitting cross-legged on the floor. Her surroundings were sparse and simple: a bamboo mat beneath her, a water basin and urn by the door, and an altar in the corner. The room was small and often dark except for the natural light that came through the one window that faced east and allowed her to know the time. That is: when to rise in the early morning before dawn, how long to sit in silent meditation, and when to greet the day and the throngs of people who came daily to worship and pray outside the temple that was her home.

Now the only sound was her own gentle, rhythmic breathing, which connected her to her inner self. She knew the value of the silence and stillness offered to her in the early hours before dawn. Her daily meditations relaxed her body, quieted her mind, and allowed her to hear the guidance she received whenever she listened carefully to her voice within. Spiraling into the universe inside her filled her with a sense of awe and wonder and connected her to all forms of life. From this place of renewed self-knowing, she began each day.

Tara achieved the self-knowledge and wisdom that the Buddhists call enlightenment. She knows and teaches that this can come only through mindful or conscious disciplines, such as the morning meditation she practiced each day. Her life had not always been as peaceful as it was today, filled with a happiness she never ceased to appreciate, for as a girl, she had faced many hardships and challenges. She had known hunger, cold, and fear. She had seen the pain of war and poverty and had lost many loved ones. Through her own life experiences she gained compassion for the pain and suffering of others, and she never tired in her efforts to offer comfort to others.

Now she sensed a calling too distant for her ears to hear. Her intuition told her there was danger and that someone needed help. Tara knew to trust such feelings, which often guided her to the right place at just the right time. She ran quickly to the nearby forest, where she often served as the protectress of man and beast. She appeared at just the right moment, for as she emerged through the trees she saw a young wood gatherer, frozen in fear, standing face-to-face with a lioness trying to protect her young. With a few soft words Tara instructed the boy to safety, gently easing his fears and kindly showing him a safer way. Then, directly and silently, she communicated her inner knowing to the agitated lioness still pacing nearby. Tara knows and shares the instincts of a mother lioness and uses her instincts and intuition to protect and guide those who need her.

Tara, the compassionate mother to her people, knew too well their fears and pain, since they had once been her own. Through work and prayer she devoted herself to easing the suffering of humankind. Now her devotees worship at her temple and invoke her name in prayer in order to receive her blessings and benefit from her power to heal all sorrows and grant all wishes.

MOTHER–DAUGHTER ACTIVITY
Tara Candle

Create a Tara candle with your daughter to remind her of Tara's wisdom. Decorate a jar of any size or shape with beads, tissue paper, and sequins. (A mixture of liquid starch and glue works well with tissue paper.) You can also create a collage around the jar using words and photos from magazines. Place a small votive or tea candle inside the jar. Light it during meditation times or use it as a reminder of your inner voice and wisdom as you go about your daily activities.

"Tara, O Blessed One, hear my prayer.
Guide me and protect me from danger.
Ease my fear and relieve my pain.
Beloved mother of compassion,
Help me gain inner wisdom and knowledge.
Lead me to peace and happiness."

◑○◐

TEACHING OUR DAUGHTERS TO BE INTUITIVE

As mothers, we set the tone for our daughters' intuitive awakenings. We all have access to a strong intuitive sense. When we are strongly connected to our own intuition, we are better able to guide our daughters in connecting and trusting their own intuition. It is simply a matter of acknowledging, trusting, and using it. Our intuition not only guides us in our own lives, but it also guides us in our relationships with our daughters. It is our intuition that cues us in when our daughters are struggling or hurting and in need of our support.

One of the biggest gifts that we can give our daughters is a sense of their own intuition. We can do that by first acknowledging and using our own intuition. Listening to and honoring their feelings teaches them to trust what they know to be true. Giving them an intuitive language encourages them to listen to their own intuitive signals and offers them the words to articulate their own perceptions and feelings. "What's your gut feeling about that? What do you sense? Do you have a hunch? What feels right to you?" Intuitive language can offer some of our best answers to our daughters' requests for advice. They can then learn to intuit and trust what they know to be right and true for themselves.

INTUITION AND BODY WISDOM

Our bodies are also vital sources of intuitive guidance. Our intuition speaks to us through our physical sensations, feelings, and reactions. Feelings of discomfort, such as sweating, increased heart rate, and fatigue, are physical responses that can contain essential information.

Many years ago I learned an intuitive technique called "the safety sensor." In a spiritual self-awareness group, my teacher asked us to imagine certain scenarios that ranged from mildly uncomfortable to downright dangerous. With each scenario, she guided us to check our bodily sensations. Our responses included sweaty palms, dry mouths, and accelerated heart rates. We learned to listen to these intuitive cues and trust that they were giving us valuable information. Our bodies can be infinitely wiser than our minds, which are often trained to please rather than to protect. Our bodies can be one of our greatest sources of intuitive wisdom.

MOTHER–DAUGHTER ACTIVITY
Safety Sensor

Guide your daughter through the safety-sensor exercise. Start from a calm and centered place by taking a few slow, deep breaths together. Then describe a few different situations that range from exciting to dangerous. These might include a public-speaking situation, the act of winning an award or race, the feeling of getting lost, or the thought of being chased by a stranger. After each scenario, ask your daughter what kinds of sensations she feels in her body. Let her know that these are her body's intuitive sensations warning her about danger. Encourage her to notice these feelings and to share them with you to strengthen her awareness. You can also practice in "real" situations. Check in at different times and ask your daughter to identify her feelings. Ask: *"What do you feel right now in your body?"* Teach her to check in with her feelings about various people, places, and situations.

As girls grow older, dolls take on new significance and their magic transcends the ages. Dolls serve as talismans and remind us of what we feel but cannot see, but they also take on the energy of their makers. With your daughter, make a doll that symbolizes intuition, the inner spirit of women and the voice of wisdom and guidance. Doll kits are available at most craft and fabric stores, but dolls can also be made from recycled Popsicle sticks, cotton balls and fabric, and a little imagination. Be creative!

We want our daughters to know and trust their intuitive feelings before they find themselves in the wrong place at the wrong time with the wrong people. Intuition is a good resource for simple or critical life decisions and choices. Where do daughters go to find the answers to their problems and dilemmas? On what do they base their own decisions and choices? Where do they look to discover what is right? Who do they turn to when we are no longer there to guide them? I want my daughter to be able to recognize and act on her feelings and her inner voice before she finds herself in dangerous situations.

There comes a time when we simply can no longer be there every moment in our daughters' lives to guide, advise, and protect them. The instincts and intuition that we have relied on to keep them safe must be handed down to them so that they can become the wise navigators on their own journeys. Intuition is one of the greatest gifts and tools that we can give our daughters to guide their own lives as they leave the safety of our protective wing and step out into the world.

The old Russian folktale of Vasalisa is a classic heroine's fairy tale that tells the story of a mother passing on the gift of intuition to her daughter.

The Doll in Her Pocket: Vasalisa the Wise

Once upon a time a young mother, whose daughter was still a child, was called to the spirit world. Before she died she lay on her deathbed, waning like the moon in her final moments of life, attended by her husband and by her daughter, Vasalisa. Her daughter knelt in prayer at her side, dressed in a white apron and red boots. As her mother drew her last breaths, she called Vasalisa to come closer to her since her voice barely a whisper.

"I have something important to give you," she breathed into her daughter's ear, "that you must always keep with you and show to no one." Vasalisa reached out her hands and received a tiny doll into her cupped fingers.

"This is for you," her mother told her, and Vasalisa saw that it was dressed exactly as she was, in red boots, a white apron, a black skirt, and a colorful embroidered vest.

"Put her in your pocket and listen carefully," said her mother. "If you should ever lose your way or need guidance or help, ask this doll what to do. She will guide and assist you. Care for her and keep her with you always. This is my final gift and promise to you, that you will always be guided. Bless you, my beloved daughter, until we meet in spirit again."

And the mother's eyes closed and her breath became still, and Vasalisa held her mother's hand for one final moment as she felt the doll inside her pocket.

◗○◖

As in many well-known fairy tales, Vasalisa's father soon remarried and receded into the background, and Vasalisa was left alone with an evil stepmother and two stepsisters, who eventually sent her off into the dark woods to meet her fate. She faced and survived many challenges, always guided by the doll her mother gave her.

The doll that Vasalisa's mother gave her represents the inner intuition and guidance of the feminine spirit. Dressed in her own likeness, the doll is Vasalisa's intuition, handed down from mother to daughter in the spirit of women. The doll in Vasalisa's pocket is the fierce instinct and life-force energy that we all carry within us. Our daughters have their own dolls in their pockets, their own instincts and intuition that they can trust and rely on. Sometimes we simply need to remind them that it is there.

LIVING AN INTUITIVE LIFE

What I have come to love most about the intuitive path is perhaps the seemingly magical synchronicities that occur along the way. An intuitive life can be full of surprises—sudden and unexpected occurrences that can help ease the journey of life. The spontaneity and wisdom of this mysterious universe often makes us smile and even laugh with amusement. Tapping into our intuition is not necessarily ominous but can bring us great joy.

The Modern-Day Tara

Today's Tara knows that her intuition is an essential source of guidance. She creates a spiritual practice that quiets her mind and allows her to listen to her inner voice. Like Vasalisa, she has been gifted by her mother with a strong sense of herself and her intuition. As she makes her way out into the world, she carries this gift with her.

3

Moon Shadow
Spending Time Alone

● ◑ ○ ◐ ●

When my friend Patti and I performed the winter-solstice ritual with our daughters (described in Chapter 1, Moon Wisdom), one of the seeds she planted was for some sacred space—a little privacy and some time and space that was her own. During the ritual we invited our wishes to show up in many and unexpected ways. Patti is a full-time teacher and mother who teaches her ten-year-old daughter, McKensey, in her fourth-grade class. They have a lot of togetherness and Patti is rarely alone, even in the car. "What I really want to do," she confided one day, "is convert our garage into an office or studio, just for me—a place where I can go to read or write that is separate from the main house and from my roles as mother and wife. But I think that's going to have to wait."

A couple of weeks into the new year, before one of our Sunday-morning walks together, Patti knocked on my door with a big smile on her face. "You won't believe what is happening," she told me. "This whole week I've been waking up easily and automatically at 4:30 in the morning. I feel rested and ready to start the day, and with everyone else still

"When a woman makes time for herself, even if it's only ten to twenty minutes a day, she will start to feel like the goddess she is meant to be. These deposits into a 'self-nurturing fund' will keep her from becoming overdrawn when she is faced with modern-day life stresses."

Cynthia Daddona,
Diary of a Modern-Day Goddess

asleep, the house is so still and quiet. I've been going into the living room and lighting a few candles and making a fire, then I've been writing in my journal, meditating, and praying. I think I've been given a sacred space."

Patti's not the only woman I know who has found solace in the wee hours of the morning. Deborah, a woman in my writing group, is also a full-time mother. One day she came into class yawning and told us that she had been regularly waking up just a little after midnight and writing until 3 A.M. "I love the night, it's when I feel most creative and inspired, and to be awake when everyone else is sleeping is magical. I feel like I have been given a divine gift. Sometimes I even feel a certain presence ... "

For those of us who love our sleep, the idea of waking up before dawn might sound like a form of torture, or just one more thing on our to-do list. After all, sleep is dreamy and restorative, and a down-comfortered, flannel-sheeted bed is, well, so heavenly. And so is sacred space—time alone, just for yourself, without the sounds of telephones, traffic, and children's voices.

"If I just had one day, one morning, one hour to myself," many busy women and mothers secretly dare to muse. "I would ... what?"

What would you do if you woke up one day and discovered that you had the whole day to yourself?

This recently happened to my friend Nancy. One Saturday morning she woke up to an empty house. She groggily realized that her husband and son, Bradley, had left for golf lessons, that her eighteen-year-old daughter, Christyn, was off on geology field study, and that Alisha, her fifteen-year-old, had spent the night at a friend's house with plans to spend the day shopping. It had been years since she had been alone at home for any extended period of time. She rolled out of bed, checked bedrooms and bathrooms to make sure she was really alone, made herself a cup of coffee, and returned to the warmth of her bed to read the paper. After a couple of hours of reading and dozing, her husband interrupted her reverie with a phone call from the golf course. He and Bradley were going to grab lunch and see the latest action movie and wouldn't be home until later in the afternoon. She smiled at her good fortune, wandered out to her garden, and spent the afternoon caring for the roses and weeding the neglect from her vegetable garden. She made a salad for lunch from the lettuce and tomatoes she had harvested. She even found time to finish the novel she had started several months earlier. Her family returned around dinnertime to find her soaking in the hot tub, relaxed and rejuvenated from her in-home retreat. What would you do with such a day? With all those "coulds" and "shoulds," and how would you discern the difference? The "coulds" are our possibilities and potentials; they are our preferences, what we hope for and long for. They are what we crave— our hearts' desires—and they are the food for our souls. The "shoulds," on the other hand, are the duties and obligations that, in large doses, eat up our time and leave our souls unnourished.

"If women were convinced that a day off or an hour of solitude was a reasonable ambition, they would find a way of attaining it," wrote Anne Morrow Lindburgh. "As it is, they feel so unjustified in their demand that they rarely make the attempt."

It's true. Spending time alone rarely shows up on our daily to-do lists.

Nancy stumbled upon, or more accurately, awakened to a day of solitude, something she might not have consciously chosen or created for herself. Even when we crave it, yearn for it, could break down and cry for it, we still push through our truths and tell ourselves, "I don't have time."

Time is the perhaps the most valuable commodity and resource in our jam-packed, overcommitted, minutely scheduled lives, and yet most of us give it away without even batting a sleepy eyelid. "Sure," we promise as we are listening to yet one more request for our time. Then we squeeze in one more half-baked obligation and put our true cravings on hold. Pretty soon, we're running on empty, delivering one more apple pie to one more soccer-club fundraiser.

Most of us create an imbalance in our lives that is greatly tipped in favor of doing rather than being, noise rather than quiet, chaos rather than stillness, and we behave as though taking time for ourselves to be alone is the supreme act of selfishness. And yet at the same time, what many of us crave most is quiet, stillness, and solitude. Like my friend Patti, we'd love a little privacy, some time alone—some sacred space. Not everyone is comfortable with solitude, nor really even all that familiar with it, though there is often an inner knowing when the time has come to retreat into a sacred space of our own.

CONSCIOUS RETREATING—PLANNING AND CREATING TIME ALONE

We all have our own natural cycles of being and doing. There are those high-energy days when we feel inspired to clean out our closets, finally finish that PowerPoint presentation the PR department has been asking for, tackle that pile of unpaid bills during lunch, and still have time to enjoy our daughters' soccer games and the pizza parties afterwards. Then there are the days when just waking up feels like a chore. There are times when we need to be reflective, taking stock and re-energizing. My friend Lynn recently had a "recuperation day." She recognized the signs of physical and mental wear and tear and stayed home, watched movies, and ate her favorite foods.

You can include your daughter in these recuperation days as well. At my house we call them "jammie days." There are days when I let Mikaila stay home from school with no other purpose than to rejuvenate. I've had to convince her that the math homework will still be there when she returns and that a day without soccer practice may do her good. Our daughters do not need to get sick before they take a break, and neither do we. A day of just being can be as productive as a day of doing, and we need to honor both.

TERRI'S RETREAT

I have never lived alone. I grew up in a big family with four siblings, and when I went off to college I always had roommates. Then I got married and started a family of my own. It wasn't until my youngest child was four years old that I went away by myself for the first time. We have friends who own a house in Cambria, a quiet surfside town on the California coast. I left on Friday and spent two luxurious nights in a quiet neighborhood surrounded by pine trees. My only visitors were a few deer that tiptoed quietly into the backyard each night at dusk. I felt like I was in a remote cabin in the woods.

What I loved the most was being able to eat and sleep according to my own natural rhythm. I ate when I was hungry and rested when I was tired. My time was my own and I followed my own inner clock. I did venture out one afternoon to walk the beach and poke around in the little boutiques and specialty shops, but mostly I cherished the quiet and restful time I spent alone. I walked along the cliffs, wandered through the quiet neighborhood, read, and napped in a house I had all to myself. It was there I realized that for the first time in my life, I was alone for more than a few hours. How could almost forty years have passed without my ever having been alone?

MOTHER–DAUGHTER ACTIVITY
The Gift of Time

For Mother's Day, your birthday, or the next special occasion, ask for the gift of time. Ask your daughter to make you several gift certificates that state the following: "This certificate entitles you to (insert time) minutes of quiet, uninterrupted time." These can be in several different increments of time, for example ten, twenty, or thirty minutes. Redeem your certificates as often as needed. Return the favor and give your daughter some gift certificates as well, offering her some privacy and uninterrupted time of her own.

I vowed that I'd return as often as possible, and I did return one more time before my private sanctuary was eventually sold to new owners. Though it took me forty years to carve out my first niche—my own sacred space—it wasn't too late. Experiences of solitude leave an imprint and create a memory that wants to be repeated. A few years later, I spent a couple of weekends at a beach retreat house just twenty minutes from my home in Santa Barbara. Though my children are older now and in many ways more self-reliant, it seems to be even harder to get away from the soccer tournaments and the busy schedules of a family of five. These days, most of my retreats take place in the early morning hours. I find solitude a few mornings a week when I get up before my children and head to the campus pool at the local university.

Discovering solitude does not need to begin with a weekend getaway. Ten minutes a day of conscious solitude is the foundation for a regular practice of spending time alone. A slow, purposeful start can be the beginning of longer and more restorative retreats.

May Sarton, Anne Morrow Lindberg, Georgia O'Keefe, and many other women have been writing for centuries now about the essential value of solitude, retreat, going away, and going within. In earlier times, nature supplied not only the backdrop for solitude, but all the materials as well. Today, as the natural world is diminished and time spent in nature becomes a smaller part of our lives, we find our own personal internal tides and instinctual cyclical rhythms severely out of whack. Once again, we turn to the goddess to lead us back to nature.

The Myth of Artemis

Artemis couldn't wait another minute. As a young goddess, she had many obligations and often visited her father Zeus on Mount Olympus. She longed to run freely across the meadow and into the forest to the clear, cool stream where she often sat in solitude, lost in her own tranquil thoughts. She had no need for conversation and in fact preferred the quiet company of animals, the silence of the moon tree, and the pebbles in the stream. So when Zeus offered her anything she desired, she asked him for independence and adventure, which he gladly granted.

Artemis had a deep connection with nature and found solace in remote places. She easily tamed the fiercest bears and befriended the most timid rabbits. And although she became a protectress of young girls, she felt more akin to animals than people, and as a young girl the animals had been her favorite playmates. She had witnessed many animals birthing in the forest and easily gained their trust, stroking the mother's head and womb as new life emerged. Later, she became a midwife, easing the pains of childbirth for the women who called on her quiet and gentle wisdom.

As a moon goddess, Artemis also understood the darkness and its mysteries. Looking into the night sky, she could see eternity and she knew that the cycle of birth and death are neverending. When the moon was new and waxing, Artemis would slip into the forest and dance freely with the animals and any mortals who dared to join her, and all was safe and well when Artemis was in the forest.

Artemis had a strong and independent feminine spirit and only fell in love once. It was her own arrow that tragically pierced the heart of her beloved, Orion. She was masterful at hunting and when her brother, Apollo, challenged her accuracy, she shot at a distant object floating in the sea. She did not recognize that the object on the horizon was her lover, Orion. The tragic loss only made the protection of the creatures she loved stronger and drew her into the forest, where she found sanctuary in remote and solitary places.

No matter what befell her, Artemis loved to spend time alone and always found solace in her own quiet company. She had a deep connection with all living things and radiated a strong sense of self. But Artemis speaks to us of independence and adventure as well. She beckons us to join her in the wilderness, to delve deeper into ourselves and find strength in the freedom of time alone.

◑◯◐

HEARING THE CALL OF ARTEMIS

Late last spring, I heard the call of Artemis and felt a strong pull to sleep outside under the moon and stars, like I had done during so many summers when I was a girl. One night at the dinner table, I announced my plan to my family. "I want to sleep outside this summer." I have of course had camping fantasies and have even been known to suggest family camping trips, but the truth is that we've never been on one. And when it comes down to sleep and comfort, there's nothing I love more than my own well-feathered nest. So I shouldn't have been all that surprised when my husband asked, "Why would you want to do that?" and my twelve-year-old daughter, Austin, simply commented, "That's interesting, Mom." But when ten-year-old Sarah's eyes lit up, I knew I had an ally, and possibly a bed.

"Sarah, how about we put your bed outside for the summer, right out on the deck under the awning. It'll be covered and protected, but we'll still able to look out into the night sky."

"Yeah," she exclaimed, and a couple of weekends later we were hauling her queen-size bed out onto our deck, flannel sheets, down comforter, and all. I wasn't looking for an Outward Bound experience or a wilderness adventure, I just wanted to move outward, comfortably, into my own backyard wilderness.

And sleeping outside with my daughters had answered the Artemis call.

My daughters and I spent many summer nights in the company of our dog and cat as well as the neighborhood raccoons, opossums, and skunks. What my daughters loved most was the sense of adventure and the feeling of risk, sleeping outside in the dark but all the while still in the safety of our own backyard. Together we gazed into the heavens, pondered the constellations, and watched millions of stars shoot across the dark night sky. We witnessed the phases of the summer moon, reveled in the brightness of the full moon, and reflected in the shadows of the new moon. Beneath a canopy of stars, we snuggled under the thick, warm covers, talked and told stories, and sometimes just listened to the sounds of nature. We talked about the vastness of the universe, the mysteries of life, and the unknowns each of us must face. Our conversations ranged from our fears and challenges to just the ordinary events of our day. Those nights together brought me back to the nights when I nursed my daughters in my grandmother's old, wooden rocking chair. It was a simple, pure connection.

And when the moon appeared, I felt that we were all watched over and protected by the Great Mother. Some nights, when I felt the cool breeze caress my cheek, I imagined that she was singing us a lullaby until we all fell asleep. Sleeping outside that summer, I felt connected to something much greater than myself; I felt exhilarated and alive.

Our backyard, back-to-nature experience didn't take us very far from home, but it did bring us all a little closer to the wild Artemis within us and to the moon above us. Later in the fall, after it started to rain, we pulled the bed back inside. But perhaps next summer we'll head out even further.

MOTHER–DAUGHTER ACTIVITY
Back to Nature

Make a date with your daughter to spend some time in nature. This could be a hike, a camping trip, or even an hour at the park. A pair of binoculars, a sketch pad and pencils, or a journal can enhance the experience. You might like to collect rocks, shells, leaves, or feathers as reminders of your outing together. Your local natural-history museum may offer classes, group outings, and other resources to help you get started.

OUR DAUGHTERS' ALONE TIME

Thirty hours a week of school, mountains of homework, after-school sports and team practices, dance classes and music lessons, weekend tournaments, mall outings, and sleepovers. Where is the downtime for our daughters, that essential self-nurturing time that allows them to replenish their inner worlds? The external lives of most coming-of-age girls today are fast-paced, busy, and loud. They have to stay up late and get up early just to squeeze it all in.

When my daughter sprained her wrist and had to quit her volleyball team, then came down with the circulating fever and flu and missed almost a full week of school, she asked me, "Do you think these things are happening to get me to slow down and stop doing so much?" I had to admit, I had to wonder.

For years, child psychologists have been talking about the dangers of expecting and imposing too much too soon and the consequent crises that occur in children and teenagers. Today the problem has only been compounded by the Internet, the media, television, and school culture.

Our daughters need time to unplug. I recently overheard a one-sided telephone conversation between a mother and daughter during which the mother, my friend Susan, was encouraging her daughter to take a break from her busy social schedule. She had spent the previous day at Disneyland, arrived home late that night, and the following morning was ready to move on to the next event. "I want you to spend some time at home," her mother told her. "You've been telling me how tired you are, and I want you to take a break." I couldn't hear her daughter's response, but I could tell that she wasn't very enthusiastic about her mother's idea. How do we convince our daughters of their own need for quiet time, when most preteen and teenage girls seem to feel the more social events and friends the better, and that being stuck at home alone is a fate worse than death? How might we encourage our daughters to set aside some quiet time, to create and appreciate downtime, and to unwind and simply "not do"?

As mothers, making room for our own downtime is essential. When we carve out our own private niche or steal a moment (or more) for ourselves, we teach our daughters by example and show them that this quiet time is as important as all the other comings and goings they witness us doing. They, too, might begin to notice and acknowledge their own inner rhythm, the natural ebb and flow of energy, the internal tide that comes and goes with the pull of the moon.

And here's where a little maternal wisdom and guidance come in. In order to swim against the current of our cultural imperative, one that heralds accomplishment, productivity, and achievement over all other ways of living, we need to help our daughters remember how to spend time alone in ways that are meaningful, enjoyable, and most importantly, self-nurturing. Our daughters need their self-nurturing funds, too, so that they don't become overdrawn by the stresses of modern-day life.

How might our daughters' lives be different if we learn to help them turn from the noise crowding in on them in order to hear their own profound silence, so that they can uncover enough time to let their whole lives emerge?

HONORING HER TIME ALONE

When Patti planted the seed for her sacred space, she was acknowledging her need for privacy, some time and space that was her own. Everyone needs and deserves a little privacy, including—and perhaps especially—our preadolescent daughters. Their bodies, minds, and souls—their inner and outer lives—are changing at rapid-fire speed, and they need time to creatively, actively, quietly, comfortably, and sometimes privately assimilate these changes. What kind of sacred space does your daughter have in her own life? How much time does she spend alone? Does she have a place to go to be alone and do special things that are hers alone? A journal is perhaps the most essential "solitude tool," and one that absolutely needs to be respected as private. If she keeps a journal, this is her place to sort out thoughts and feelings, to voice her confusion and clarify her truths. It's her special place to dream and imagine, to create fantasies that she may or may not ever play out. And that's what solitude, privacy, retreating, and sacred space are about.

My thirteen-year-old daughter and her friend Jordan recently went on a "vision quest" as a part of their coming-of-age program. One of the requirements of the weekend was that each participant come prepared to spend two hours alone. Jordan dreaded the thought of that amount of alone time and even concocted some strategies to avoid it. When the time came, Jordan reluctantly gathered her journal, a backpack with a granola bar, a water bottle, and a whistle to signal if she needed help. She set off from camp and settled under a tree next to a creek to begin her inner journey. The next morning, Jordan told the coming-of-age group that the two hours she had spent alone had been a "gift" and that she was surprised at how much she liked and needed it. "I would have never imagined that being alone could have been so great," she said. "I actually liked being with myself in the quiet of nature. I'm ready to do it again." Jordan needed a scheduled opportunity to experience true solitude for the first time. Words like "solitude," "downtime," and "quiet" have taken on a whole new meaning for Jordan. A similar quiet-time plan can help our own daughters discover that same gift of solitude.

CREATING PERSONAL ALTARS

Personal altars can be visible reminders of the value of spending quiet time alone. The girls in the moon groups loved creating personal altars. These creative projects began as raw-pine boxes, about twelve inches high and six inches wide, with a cut-out moon shape on the top. The girls covered their altar with splashes of watercolors, shiny beads, colorful baubles, and streaks of glitter. Each box was as unique as the girl who made it. An altar, when made by hand or adorned with personal objects, is like a mirror that reflects the essence of its creator. The girls placed little angel figurines, clay goddesses, and candles inside, along with some other favorite personal objects. Their personal altars served as reminders of the importance of quiet, reflective time alone.

The simple act of placing or creating an altar on a table-top, bookshelf, or windowsill defines that space as sacred and invites spiritual awareness and intention. Sometimes we create altars and sacred spaces without even consciously knowing it.

The word altar comes from the Latin *alta*, meaning "high place." The word referred to the physical places where altars were originally placed, such as hilltops outside or mantles inside homes, as well as the higher realm they typically represented. A home altar creates a sacred space for prayer and reflection. It can be a reminder to ask for guidance or to show gratitude for blessings.

LIKE MOTHER, LIKE DAUGHTER:
MCKENSEY'S CLUBHOUSE

Not too long after Patti planted her seed of intention for sacred space, her ten-year-old daughter, McKensey, presented her with a proposal for a clubhouse. She began her proposal by saying, "I was staring out the window and saw a desolate

---

MOTHER–DAUGHTER ACTIVITY
Personal Altars

Help your daughter find a personal space in her room (a windowsill, private corner, shelf, or dresser top) or in the backyard where she can create an altar. In her altar she can include shells, rocks, feathers, figurines, photographs, or some of her other favorite objects. And you might like to create one for yourself, as well. Remember that an altar is like a mirror in that it reflects who you are. Notice which objects you each choose. Talk about each object and discuss what makes it special to you. Visit your altars daily, perhaps first thing in the morning or right before bed, and take a few moments for quiet reflective time.

place on the side of the house and I had a vision, a vision of me and my friends building a clubhouse under a baby-blue sky and white, puffy clouds that looked like marshmallows." The proposal went on to describe windows, stepping-stone pathways, and ideas for the interior design. She even offered to raise money for accessories and furniture for the playhouse.

Patti, having just found a way to create space for herself, recognized her daughter's desire. Even though McKensey has a room of her own and plenty of privacy, she was looking for another place, separate from the main house, her own sacred outdoor space, a place in nature in which she could get away, dream, and imagine. So Patti and McKensey took action. They worked together to create preliminary plans and drawings for the clubhouse. Patti talked a good friend of the family into building it on Saturdays, promising him homemade lunches and dinners as he worked. To finance the gossamer fairy curtains for the clubhouse windows, McKensey set up a rickety card table on the corner and sold lemonade and brownies to neighbors. As I write this, McKensey's vision is on its way to becoming a reality, complete with long summer days and flashlight sleepovers in a space all her own. Artemis is alive and well in McKensey.

The Modern-Day Artemis

The Artemis of today is as comfortable in nature as she is in cyberspace. She is aware of her own natural rhythm and seeks to balance her active and busy life with healthy doses of downtime. She knows that creating time to rest and restore her energy are essential to her well-being, and that spending quiet time alone replenishes her inner world and nourishes her soul. She has an independent spirit and radiates a strong sense of self.

4

Moon Wind
Finding Your Voice

●◗○◖●

My twelve-year-old daughter, Austin, started seventh grade this year and went from a small elementary school tucked away in a close-knit, family-oriented community to a large, centrally located junior high school with kids from eight different elementary schools all over town. Her natural shyness was instantly amplified. For the first time, making new friends and meeting new people became at once an overwhelming challenge and a priority based on "social survival." For the first three months I struggled with her, trying to decide if I could best help her by encouraging her to accept her own true nature—quiet and observant—or by teaching her new skills to help "put herself out there."

"It's okay to be shy, and making new friends takes time and practice," I reassured her. "And it's okay to be a little uncomfortable for a while when moving from one comfort zone to another."

"No, it's not okay to be shy," she informed me. "Everyone else knows how to talk to new people, except me!"

I decided that, though self-acceptance is essential, we needed to move on and make some headway into overcoming

"Girls who are free-thinking and expressive, who speak their minds and hearts, suddenly begin to lose their voices and become silent."

Virginia Beane Rutter,
Celebrating Girls

her shyness. During winter break, she spent her downtime online, chatting with acquaintances from school. By the time her vacation was over, she was eager to go back to school to continue chatting with her newfound friends. But after her first day back from winter break, she came home and told me her day was "wretched."

"Everyone was talking to other people at lunch and I couldn't think of anything to say. I felt like a loner. It was so much easier online."

Okay, these are not words that a mother wants to hear, nor the image she wants to hold of her own precious daughter at a big, public junior high. I spent the next couple of days thinking about how I could help her gain new confidence in her ability to express herself and let people know how interesting, fun, and fabulous she really is. If I could just give her something to take with her, a dose of confidence, a lucky charm, a bracelet, or something—and then I remembered Oya.

Oya, an African goddess from Yoruba, is the patroness of leadership and is called upon to help with communication, especially during conflict.

The Myth of Oya

The West African girls of the Yoruba village chattered and bantered with each other as they headed for the doorway of the large thatched-roof hut, but left their jokes outside when they came to receive the teachings of Oya. Though Oya loved and cared deeply for all the children of Yoruba, teaching the girls to communicate powerfully and confidently was serious business, and Oya demanded and commanded respect. Oya was a powerful warrior who often joined her husband, Shango, in battle.

Oya is one of the most powerful *orishas*, or deities, in Africa. As goddess of the wind, she can be as gentle as a warm summer breeze or as vicious as a mighty tornado. She knows how to persuade and charm with words, and relies on her strong intuition to choose her words carefully. Oya is known amongst the Yoruba as the patroness of female leadership, and the women often ask her for help in finding the right words to resolve conflicts and gain power. They call upon Oya to teach their daughters the power of words and confident communication.

Each day when the girls came for their lesson, they brought an offering for Oya and placed it on the altar in the corner of the room. Their offerings included *akara* (her favorite bean cakes), *obi* (kola nuts), *epo pupo* (palm oil), plantains, grape wine, and *oti* (gin).

First, Oya taught the girls to speak with their bodies. She instructed the girls to always stand tall, hold their heads high, and make eye contact with both their friends and enemies. She implored them to never look down or away from the target of their words or actions.

Through chanting and drumming, Oya instructed them in the power of pure sound. She taught them to call up their own powerful sounds from deep within their bellies, raising the energy and carrying it through their hearts, throats, and lips. She also taught them to attune their voices to the sound of the drums, strong and low. When the girls had mastered the art of powerful sound, she gave them the strongest words she knew, to use in any situation. Though a harsh and demanding teacher, Oya was a fierce and loyal protectress. She was proud of her girls. She taught them to use their words and power to clear away injustice, to resolve conflict, and to always speak the truth.

The girls always left her hut with their heads held high, singing and rejoicing in their power, dressed in multicolored cloths of maroon, orange, burgundy, copper, and dark red, well equipped for any battle with their own arsenals of charms and magic.

◗○◗

I live near a shop that carries spiritual books, tapes, jewelry, statues, and goddess figurines. They also have an assortment of gemstones that come with a card listing the special qualities attributed to each stone. One day I was sifting through the stones and reading the descriptions of their purposes. I looked at amethyst "for connection to your higher self," rose quartz for "compassion and an open heart," and moon stone for "female issues and changes." Then I discovered blue lace agate: "Reduces introversion; enhances creativity and confident expression; reduces stress." Bingo! That's the one for Austin, I thought, as I caressed the small, smooth stone and headed for the cash register.

That night, before Austin went to bed, I pulled out the stone and presented it to her, telling her about its properties. "I think the stones work if you believe in them; that is, if you believe in the possibilities they offer, and especially in the possibilities within yourself. Keeping it in your pocket might serve as a reminder that, like this stone, you have the capacity for confident expression. I don't think it's necessarily going to do it for you, I think you have to work with it."

My daughter is getting used to my magical rituals and beliefs and is a good sport—plus, at this point she seemed willing to try anything. The next day she put the smooth blue stone into her pocket and headed for the jungle.

As I dropped her off at school, I took a breath and said a little prayer to Oya.

When I picked her up from school that day, she headed for my car with a big smile on her face. "Mom," she asked, "can I go home with Nikki today?" I knew who Nikki was because Austin had told me that she was someone she wanted to make friends with, but had been too shy to invite her over to the house.

"Is it okay with her mom?" I asked, then went through my usual list of questions. "Who's going to be there? What's her address and phone number? Call me when you get there, and," I smiled back at her, "have a great time."

So do these stones really have the special properties and magical powers that create changes in a single day? Or are they just interesting to look at and nice to hold? What I believe is that I had offered my daughter an opportunity, not so much to believe in the power and possibility of a stone, but to believe in her own possibilities for confident expression. The stone was simply a reminder of this. I think that that is the true magic—the belief in your own "Oya power" and in yourself—and sometimes we just need a way to remember.

WHAT IS CONFIDENT EXPRESSION?

For my daughter, confident expression meant finding her voice and using it to put herself out there and make new friends. When asked, women I know describe confident expression as "the ability to speak with ease and fluidity in any situation to any number of people; it means speaking one's truth regardless of the consequence and being authentic and true to oneself." For one woman, it meant being able "to sing from my soul!"

If you don't have it, how do you get it? Sometimes it comes from self-acceptance, but it might take a cosmic gift, and it definitely takes practice.

In *Rami's Book, The Inner Life of a Child*, the eleven-year-old author tells a story about finding her voice. Rami and her mother came up with a point system to help her with her shyness, in which she would earn points every time she spoke to someone outside her family. The same day of their agreement, Rami broke her arm while camping. A few days later, she and her family left on a trip to visit her grandparents. Everywhere she went—to the airport, restaurants, and on family excursions—people asked about her cast. She earned sixty points just describing how she broke her arm. In the process, she forgot all about her shyness and discovered that it was actually fun to talk.

"The night before my cast was to be taken off," writes Rami, "I rubbed my arm and cast lovingly. I felt the broken arm had really helped me a lot. I realized that there had been a great hidden blessing for me in breaking my arm. There must be a hidden blessing in everything that seems bad."

The point system worked for Rami and the special stones helped Austin find her voice. In each instance, these girls felt shy and unable to speak. But once they started talking they found that, like the friend in Austin's story or the people Rami met in her story, people do actually want to hear their stories. They learned that practice and sometimes something outside of themselves, such as the stone and the arm cast, provided a little external support or incentive that helped them overcome their shyness. We all know girls who seem to have no problem talking but quite often struggle to find the right words. In early adolescence, it is especially hard to articulate what you want, need, or are trying to say. As mothers, how can we learn to teach our daughters to communicate clearly, honestly, and kindly, with respect for others and themselves?

CHOOSING THE RIGHT WORDS— ASSERTIVE COMMUNICATION

When you speak from your heart, your statements are automatically authentic and true. Speaking from the heart is also a natural form of assertive communication.

Remember the scene from *Fried Green Tomatoes* in which Kathy Bates's character, Evelyn, after some assertiveness training, rams her car into someone else's in the grocery-store parking lot to prove that she can stick up for herself? Though you have to love Evelyn as she evolves into her new self, ramming her car is hardly an assertive act. It's aggression, something many of us learned during the early stages of assertiveness training. But true assertiveness honors individual rights and equality in relationships. Assertiveness allows us to choose for ourselves, to stand up for ourselves without anxiety, to express honest feelings comfortably, and to enhance our own feelings of self-worth as well as those of others.

The key to developing assertive behavior is to practice—practice listening, watching, thinking, feeling, and responding. It is not something that necessarily comes naturally to most people. In our culture, "good girls" are often defined as quiet and obedient, which is a passive style of behavior. A girl can be assertive and still be a "good" person; in fact, she can be a better person because she is honest with herself and others. Believing that you must assert yourself in all situations is not necessary—you have the right to choose how, when, and whether to respond. We can teach our daughters to be assertive by making sure they know that their feelings and opinions are valid. They need to know that it is okay to disagree, say no, and change their minds. We can let them know that we will be there to support them and that it is okay to ask for help in difficult situations. In fact, just asking for help is an assertive act. If we treat our daughters with respect, we can show them how to respect others and teach them that they deserve respect from others as well. Respect for diversity and other points of view is essential to having meaningful, assertive conversations and relationships. It is probably unrealistic to think that your daughter will read a book or attend a class on assertiveness training, but practicing clear communication with her is an essential first step.

Our emotions are a powerful source of authentic and heartfelt expression. With your daughter identify six of your strongest emotions. These might include joy, sadness, or anger. Collect some smooth or flat stones and paint them the colors that express each feeling. Then write one of your emotions on each stone. Let these stones remind you of the value of acknowledging and expressing your feelings. You might also like to describe something in nature that represents each emotion. For example: "My anger is like thunder."

Assertive communication is honest, kind, and respectful. By beginning with simple "I" statements and progressing to more complex forms of communication and self-expression, we can be more aware of the power of words. With a greater awareness of our own personal communication style, we can learn to choose the right words in order to express ourselves in many different kinds of situations. Passive, aggressive, and assertive methods are the three primary ways in which we can respond to a situation. Passive communicators rely on hints and whining, aggressive communicators yell and threaten, but assertive communicators are honest and straightforward.

Knowing that your daughter has a ton of homework and finding her watching TV can evoke a number of responses. Sighing and leaving the room without saying anything is passive. "Turn that damn thing off. You are wasting your time and you'll never get your homework finished!" is accusatory and aggressive. "I'm worried you will run out of time to finish, I would like you to turn the TV off and get started on your homework. I'm available to help you with your homework," is assertive and a better place to start. She may still resist turning off the TV and getting her work finished, but if she does she will not be reacting solely to your words. Statements that begin with phrases like "I would like," "I feel," "I choose," "I need," or "I believe" are good starters. And it isn't always easy—there are going to be plenty of times when frustration and fear take over and your communication ends with yelling and slamming bedroom doors. Acknowledging our own mistakes and apologizing when it's appropriate are assertive acts, too. For more information on good communication skills, your local library, adult-education classes, or counseling centers can also be good resources. And don't give up—remember that it does take practice.

In her book *Reviving Ophelia*, Mary Pipher writes, "Communication with teenage daughters encourages rational thought, centered decisions, and conscious choices. It includes discussions of opinions, risks, implications, and consequences. Parents can teach their daughters to make choices. They can help them sort out when to negotiate, stand firm, and withdraw. They can help them sort out what they can and can't control, how to pick their battles, and to fight back. They can teach intelligent resistance."

My friend Jody has two well-spoken adolescent daughters who are thirteen and fifteen. At a time when most girls tend to lose their voices, Rachel and Rose are still able to speak their own truths. I give Jody a lot of credit for this because she doesn't let them off the hook. She doesn't take "I don't know" (which is easily one of the most frequently spoken phrases of preteen and adolescent girls) for an answer. Jody knows that her daughters do know how they think and feel. Jody has a strong voice of her own and could easily speak for her daughters by putting her words and opinions in their mouths. Instead, Jody uses her strength to listen to and encourage her daughters to use their own voices and express their own feelings and opinions. Jody also teaches them to own those feelings and desires. I recently witnessed one of Jody's strategies. Rachel came into the kitchen and asked, "Emma wants me to go to the playground with her and Owen. May I go?" Jody looked at Rachel and gently asked, "What?" Rachel paused, smiled, and said, "I want to go the playground with Emma and Owen. May I?" A subtle but powerful difference. Jody is teaching her daughters to express themselves assertively and confidently.

COMMUNICATION AND THE WRITTEN WORD

Writing is also a tool for confident expression. Many women today are finding their voices through writing. For the last

When we connect with our own voice through writing, we are able to connect authentically with others. Write your daughter a short and simple letter that requires an answer. Be sure to pick a topic of interest, and one that requires her to offer her opinions or feelings. For example, ask her what she thinks of the dress code or other rules at her school. Ask her to write back to you. E-mail is great for this!

few years, I have been facilitating weekly writing groups for women and I've had the privilege of witnessing this phenomenon up close and personal. Women who believe they have nothing unique or interesting to say are learning to connect with their authentic selves through simple and easy writing exercises, thereby discovering truths and voices within that they had never heard before. Writing reminds us who we really are. As we lay down words on paper, we begin to see our true selves reflected back. Women's journals can be clear and powerful mirrors.

For many girls and women, writing is a more comfortable way to express strong feelings, to articulate thoughts, or to clarify ideas. Writing offers a way to express thoughts and feelings to another person without being interrupted. In many ways, writing offers us the safety of expressing our feelings in the privacy of a personal journal. It also offers us the chance to clarify and refine our feelings, and sometimes it is just an outlet for thoughts that never need to leave the page. Occasionally, writing is the only form of expression that feels safe. And a thoughtfully written letter or card is assertive, too. I always tell the women in my groups that when developing a writing practice, even five minutes a day is enough. And it is.

YOU NEVER LISTEN TO ME

The day started off as usual, I slugged down a quick cup of coffee, enough fuel to awaken my foggy brain and begin to coordinate the day's events—specifically, who needed to be where, in which uniform, with what instrument, and when. Will had karate practice at 3:30, Emma's violin lesson started at 4:00, and Mikaila had her first high-school soccer game somewhere in between. I hopped in the shower—my own private think tank—where I could mentally go over the day's schedule. Mikaila walked in and yelled over the shower door, "So what time are you coming to school?"

"I don't know yet, call me on my cell phone when you know when you get out of school."

I hurriedly dried myself off and grabbed for the clothes on my chair, and Mikaila asked again, "So what time are you coming?"

Exasperated, I raised my voice and said, "I don't know. It depends on how the afternoon goes."

As mothers we spend a lot of time talking. We arrange schedules, collect information, and give directions. Sometimes I don't really hear my daughters' questions. Before her ride came, it occurred to me that what she was really asking me was to be there. She simply wanted me to be there. It seems so obvious in retrospect, but I hadn't taken time to listen to her words and, more importantly, what was behind those words. So I backed the conversation up and said, "What time would you like me to come to your game?" With a sigh of relief, she said, "My game starts at 3:15." Rearranging my afternoon schedule was worth the trouble so I could be available for her.

An essential ingredient to clear and open communication is listening. We are much more inclined to use our authentic voices and to express our true feelings and opinions when we feel that they are respected and that we are really being listened to. Listening to and encouraging our daughters' voices strengthens their intuition and inner wisdom.

Listening without advising, problem solving, or redirecting takes time and patience. Our busy lives seem to leave little time for authentic listening, and the hardest time to listen is when we are tired, busy, or in a hurry. Oftentimes, this is when our daughters want our attention the most—when they sense that we are distracted and unavailable to them. Their interruptions are often their way of getting the assurance they need that we really are there for them, even when it doesn't look or feel like it.

MOTHER–DAUGHTER ACTIVITY
Talking Stick

Give your daughter some kind of talking stick, basket, or bowl. It could also be a shell or a stone. Let her know that this gift symbolizes the gift of listening, and that she can come to you with it the next time she wants your undivided attention and some uninterrupted listening.

THE LOST ART OF LISTENING:
ANCIENT COUNCIL CIRCLES

In our hurry-up culture and busy lives, we have forgotten how to listen. In the homeschooling program in which I teach, we use an ancient tradition called "council circle" to facilitate speaking and listening. In council circles, there is no hierarchy and each person sits in an equal position of power. Although a couch and chairs are available, we make a circle sitting on the floor. Before we start, I remind the group of a few basic rules established by the Native American council circles from whom we borrowed this technique: be brief and succinct, tell the truth, speak from your heart, and listen respectfully. In many council circles, a talking stick is used to identify the person who is speaking. When someone is holding the talking stick, no one else may speak, interject, or interrupt. Women's council circles often use a more female object in place of the stick, such as a smooth, round stone or a shell. During these circles, the students not only have a space to speak, but they also have a place to listen and be listened to. I know families who have adopted the practice of the council circle and use it when they wish to speak together about matters of importance.

Council circles and facilitated discussion groups offer adolescents an opportunity to gain self-awareness and self-confidence. Their peers can offer not only the comfort of shared and common experiences, but can also provide a place to practice effective communication skills. Guided conversations that employ ground rules and prearranged agreements can provide a safe container for the complex feelings, emotions, and struggles of adolescence. Learning these skills will exponentially contribute to positive communication well beyond the teen years and into adulthood.

A valuable guide for me has been *Talk With Teens About Self and Stress—50 Guided Discussions for School and Counseling Groups*, by Jean Sunde Peterson. She offers this advice: "The purpose of these guided discussion groups is to serve the affective need of adolescent students. Through the groups students can gain self-awareness, and that in turn helps them to make better decisions, solve problems, and deal more effectively with their various environments. They learn to affirm themselves in all of their complexity and they feel more in control of their lives. It may be enough to say that the purpose of these groups is simply to let students express themselves—to 'just talk.' They need practice putting words to their feelings and concerns. As much as some of them talk socially, they may not be skilled at communicating their feelings honestly and with clarity. Later in life, their relationships and their employment will all be enhanced if they are able to talk about what is important to them. Adolescence is a good time to learn those skills."

She continues: "In the affective realm, students have much in common. Everyone is navigating the uneven seas of adolescence, with complex feelings, frustrations, and anxieties and without the skills to ensure smooth sailing. Discussion groups can provide a place for safe talk about this journey."

Postscript

A few weeks after I gave Austin the blue lace agate stone, she climbed into my car after school and informed me that she'd lost it.

"At school?" I queried.

"Maybe," she bemused. "It must have fallen out of my pocket."

"That's interesting," I commented. "What do you make

MOTHER–DAUGHTER ACTIVITY
Council Circle

Council circles are a great way to facilitate discussion groups of all kinds. Help start a "council circle" at your daughter's school, church, Girl Scout meeting, or any other place where girls gather in a group. The gathering can be informal, as well. For example, you can use it the next time your daughter's soccer team needs to agree on a team name. You can even use the soccer ball as the talking stick.

of that?" She is used to me looking for the deeper meaning in situations, so she stopped to consider my question for a moment.

"I guess I don't need it anymore," she concluded.

"I was thinking the same thing," I told her. And together we wondered aloud who might put it in their pocket next.

The Modern-Day Oya

The modern-day Oya speaks clearly and confidently from her heart. She acknowledges her true feelings and expresses them authentically. She knows her personal rights and expresses herself assertively. She values being listened to and listening to others. Her relationships with others are kind, honest, and respectful.

5

Moon Dreams

Exploring Your Dreams

●○○●●

My friend Nona is a dream artist; she's also an intuitive massage therapist and shamanic healer, but we don't usually acknowledge that last thing beyond tightly closed doors, since it can sound a little weird. But she's been an extraordinary dreamer all of her life and can slip in and out of dream states with remarkable ease.

She recently moved from a funky old beach cottage to a rustic and sprawling house in the woods, and I couldn't wait to see her new place. She sleeps in a dormered attic room beneath a big window looking out to giant native oak trees, sunrises and sunsets, and the night sky, which was a perfect spot for us to talk about dreams.

"When I was growing up," Nona told me, "and beginning to explore my independence, it was my mother who I would go to when I wanted to secure a new privilege. She was certainly more approachable and most often willing to say yes. She understood my desire to shave legs that weren't all that hairy, and to wear a bra, even if I didn't need one yet. Getting my ears pierced, though, apparently required a little more thought. 'Let me sleep on it,' she would say,

> "Dreams are ... illustrations from the book your soul is writing about you."
>
> Marsha Norman

Dream Wisdom

whenever my question required a little more consideration. 'Sleeping on it' meant not only having time to think, but also allowing for the wisdom of dream time to incubate a thought. I used to think she was just stalling, trying to buy time perhaps, hoping I might forget about it or move on to an easier request. I didn't understand that she was consciously, or even unconsciously, calling on the wisdom of her dreams. Looking back, it's not all that surprising, even if it wasn't her conscious intention. I've been a prolific dreamer my whole life, whether I'm awake or asleep," she added with a laugh.

"Even though my mom wasn't advising me to sleep on it, she must have had some unconscious knowing of this ancient dream art, and without realizing it, I learned it from her. I've been remembering and recording my dreams since I was a little girl."

Nona leads a weekly women's dream circle, and the participants bring their nighttime dreams to the group to share. During the group, the women don't attempt to analyze or interpret each other's dreams—they simply share and listen to them. When women come to the group for the first time, they often fear that they won't have any dreams to share. But everyone dreams, every night. It just takes practice to remember those dreams. According to sleep and dream studies, everyone has four or five dreams a night. Your last dream in the early morning hours is usually the longest dream and the easiest one to remember. You may have to be willing to linger in bed for awhile after you wake up, but before you are fully awake you can usually pull that last dream through from your sleeping unconscious mind to your wakeful conscious mind, even if it's only in bits and pieces. Dream fragments can be as informative as full dreams, and you really only need to be able to remember a few words or images in order to benefit from the dream.

In the dream group, participants share with each other different ways of remembering and enhancing dreams.

Nona believes that the environment around your bed can really affect your dream life. She tries to keep it open and uncluttered, sometimes putting something specific by her bed—a little object symbolizing something if she wants to have a dream that will guide her through a certain area of her life. She sleeps with a dream pillow made of Chinese silk brocade and filled with lavender for inspiration, peppermint for fragrance, and mugwort for protection in the dream state and to promote vivid dreaming.

Sometimes she also puts a little nutmeg, which is said to be a mild hallucinogenic, in her coffee in the morning or in her tea at night, but simply keeping a dream journal by your bed can create a powerful intention to remember your dreams. Nona also recommends writing a letter to your dreamer, with a specific request for special help or assistance. Many ancient cultures had special prayers and prayer rituals that they used to induce certain and specific types of dreams.

During our conversation, Nona gave me a dream pillow, a dream prayer, and some nutmeg, so I couldn't wait to get home. The sun had set behind the oak trees, so I was beginning to feel like an invader in Nona's dreamscape and was eager to get started on creating my own.

I gathered up my treasures, said a grateful good-bye, and headed into the night, off to meet the dream goddess.

The Myth of the Dreaming Goddess

Long ago and faraway, on the island of Malta, a powerful goddess existed that possessed the ability to heal others through dreams. Those who knew of her healing gifts and powers would make pilgrimages from far and wide to receive her blessing and make offerings at her temples. These temples were usually underground and contained an elaborate system of many intricate caverns carved and rounded in the earth and painted red. They were shaped in the form of the goddess's body, with her womb as a central chamber that was used during the healing rituals. The petitioners would purify themselves and journey to her temple, then sleep inside her cavern and pray for a healing dream.

Adriana had heard of these caverns since she was a little girl. The time had come to visit this powerful goddess and receive her blessings, so she wrapped her meager belongings in a scarf and began her journey. Adriana was troubled by the feuding of her husband and his brothers and needed the advice of the wise goddess. Before she reached the caves, she bathed in the stream nearby, using the sweet herbs growing nearby to cleanse and anoint herself. She entered the cave timidly, found her way to the central chamber, said a prayer to the goddess, and fell asleep. That night her head was full of images of abundance—fields of wheat growing tall and strong, sheep by the hundreds grazing on hills of neverending green. In the early morning light, the goddess came to her and told her of the fortunes that would come to her family if they honored each other and worked together. She told Adriana that if the brothers believed in each other there would always be enough for the family. Adriana thanked the goddess, left her an offering, and returned home.

She told her husband and his brothers about the advice that the goddess had given her. That night, after the brothers had prayed to the goddess, the rain came. Ewes gave birth to lambs and the goddess of fortune smiled upon Adriana and her family.

Although Adriana never returned to the caves of the dreaming goddess, the goddess continued to visit her in the night, offering advice and the ability to look inside her soul for answers.

◑○◑

Pictures and images depicting the dreaming goddess have been found carved into the rock inside caves throughout the Mediterranean. She is also depicted in clay statues and figurines, lying on her right side with her hand under her head, in the Tibetan yoga pose believed to induce powerful dreaming.

Dream incubation is an ancient art that has been practiced by many cultures around the world, including the ancient Egyptians and Greeks, the Tibetans, the Malaysian Senoi, Native Americans, and contemporary Indians. In some cultures, the dream incubation ceremony is a shamanic journey used to connect the conscious and unconscious minds and access the wisdom of the superconscious, or universal mind. It was used as a method of transformation by which the traveler could enter into the dark unknown and bring the divine mysteries and wisdom back into waking life.

MOTHER–DAUGHTER ACTIVITY
Dream Prayer

Invite your daughter to join you in writing a prayer to your own inner dreamer—your "dream goddess"—then create a bedtime ritual using this prayer. You can use the following sample prayer, given to me by Nona, as a guide, but your own prayer should be written in your own words:

Dear Dream Self,

Thank you for all the wisdom you have offered me through my dreams, even when I might not have noticed. I feel your loving presence both in the dream of the night and the dream that unfolds in the daylight.

I ask of you tonight to bring me a dream—a dream of power, a dream of strength, a dream of clarity—so that I might know which path to go on and which direction to surrender myself to.

I ask for your guidance this night so that I may celebrate tomorrow's new day.

With love and gratitude,

(Your Name)

Make a dream pillow with your daughter. You will need scissors; a needle and a spool of thread; soft fabric such as cotton, velvet, flannel, silk, or satin; soft stuffing such as batting, cotton, or feathers; and dried herbs and flowers. Fill the pillow with lavender for inspiration, peppermint for fragrance, and mugwort for protection during the dream state and to promote vivid dreaming. Before going to sleep, place it inside your regular pillow and say a prayer to remember your dreams. Sweet dreams!

LISTENING TO OUR DAUGHTERS' DREAMS

Dreams can be especially vivid and powerful during certain life passages and cycles and even more useful during times of transformation and change. Many indigenous cultures place a strong emphasis on dreaming, especially at the time of a girl's first period. Dreams that occur at this time often are used to predict the future and guide the life of the dreamer. There are many rituals and ceremonies that are believed to inspire and enhance dreaming.

In almost all Native American tribes the vision quest is a coming-of-age ritual used to induce a dream or vision revealing a young person's special gifts and life purpose. The vision quest is essentially another form of dream incubation. After a preparatory ritual or purification ceremony, a young person would be sent off into the wilderness or a special tent to be alone for several days, while they waited for a visit from the spirit world in the form of a dream or vision. Once they received their vision, they would return to the tribe and share it with the elders, who would identify their life's purpose from the dream. (You can read more about vision quests in Chapter 12.)

THE DREAMER

Native American dreamers, like ancient dreamers all over the world, are endlessly encouraged to dream, beginning in childhood. Children are encouraged to dream in order to enhance their creativity and intuitive self-knowing, and to consciously create their lives.

In ancient times, "dreamers" were recognized in almost every culture. Because of their extraordinary gift for dreaming and connecting with the spiritual realm, this was their job and role in their community. Held in reverence, they dreamed the collective vision for their village or tribe, and they also listened to and interpreted individual dreams. Their dreams often foresaw otherwise unforeseeable events and thereby prevented calamity and danger. They also offered a vision of how to live in balance and harmony with nature and each other. Today, dreamers continue to live amongst us, though they are not always recognized for the creative and intuitive gifts they offer, and few people know how they come about them.

I live with such a dreamer. As a baby, my daughter Sarah took long, restful naps and at nighttime slept deeply and peacefully. She still loves her bed and doesn't like to get up too quickly in the morning. On a recent school morning, I glanced at the kitchen clock and decided I had better call her to breakfast. She had gotten up earlier, but after passing once through the kitchen, had climbed back into bed. I looked into her room and saw her in bed with her eyes closed. "Sarah, you'd better get up," I called from the doorway. She smiled, but kept her eyes closed. "Just a few more minutes," she whispered. "I'm still in my dream."

Like my friend Nona, Sarah spends a lot of active time in her dream state, during the night as well as the day. She's highly creative and captures her imagination through all kinds of art, but she especially loves to draw. Though she is a bright and capable child, she doesn't always finish her classwork on time. This year her teacher told me that Sarah spends a lot of time daydreaming before she starts her work. Sarah is a dreamer and like most dreamers, she needs time to dream up her ideas and her visions. This doesn't always work out, though, given her limited class time. According to my friend Rachelle, a teacher in an independent home-based school program in Ojai, California, Sarah has a distinctive learning style known as the "creative thinker." Creative thinkers need longer stretches of time to "sit and wonder" before they can jump into an assignment. They need time to dream up their ideas and processes. Though they are often negatively identified as daydreamers in class, they are usually highly creative individuals, and unless they have creative time somewhere in their lives, they often shut down and are not able to shine. For them, dreaming is an invaluable source of inspiration and perhaps their best medicine.

SUPPORTING OUR DAUGHTERS' DREAMS

According to most dream experts, we all have the ability and wisdom to create our own modern-day dream incubation and induction practice, right in our very own beds.

Some of us are more naturally connected to our dreaming mind and are able to enter our dream time with greater ease. If we have the intention, we can all have the power to induce and remember beneficial dreams and be guided and assisted by their wisdom. After all, we all dream.

But for those of us who are not as easily connected to our dreaming selves, there are strategies and techniques that we can use. Like the women in Nona's groups, we can offer our daughters dream pillows and journals to help them induce and remember dreams.

For our daughters, believing in the power of their own dreams is what empowers their creativity, intuition, and imagination. We can help by listening to their sleeping dreams and supporting their waking dreams. Offering our daughters the "treasures" to enhance their dreams and the tools to call on and remember them is one of the ways we can support their own coming-of-age wisdom and inner knowing. And it begins with believing in the magic and power of dreams.

I often hear my daughters talking with each other and their friends about their dreams, particularly after a sleep-over. They laugh about and ponder the weirdness of the characters and events that transpire in their dreams. They compare notes with each other and do a little amateur analyzing of each other's dreams. The dream of climbing Mount Everest might mean that they will do well on that geometry final. My sixteen-year-old daughter recently dreamt that she woke up to find a powder-blue Jeep in our driveway—just for her! Almost every teen driver wishes for their own car because it represents independence—the opportunity to come and go as they please and in a vehicle other than the old station wagon with the dents and the six-digit odometer. And the powder-blue Jeep? A symbol of freedom with a touch of creativity and class!

The Art of Dreaming~
Activities for Creative Dream Play

In her book *The Art of Dreaming—Tools for Creative Dream Work*, Jill Mellick offers many imaginative and inspiring ideas for exploring and expressing dreams. She suggests the following:

1. Turn your dream into a fairy-tale beginning with "Once upon a time ..."
2. Make a poem out of a dream.
3. After you write it down, rewrite it as a poem. Try haiku.
4. Draw a dream mandala. A mandala is a picture within a circle that tells a whole story.
5. Re-enact your dream movements. Use mime to express what words cannot.
6. Move like your dream animal, starting with shape and even adding sound.
7. Use collage to express color, shape, and theme.
8. Make masks of dream figures.
9. Use clay to express feeling, movement, and figure.
10. Create energy paintings.

AND DON'T FORGET TO NAP

Many of us know the restorative value of napping.
Sometimes a quick catnap of fifteen minutes can help us
make it through those pesky PTA meetings or a two-hour
recital of beginning violinists. A nap can also free our creative mind when we are really stuck. I know that when I am
at the computer writing and the words refuse to come, a
quick ten- or fifteen-minute nap—preceded by a meditation
in which I call on the dream goddess for help—can open the
gates to my more productive and creative subconscious. I
can then return to my computer, ignore the call of solitaire,
and write again with a renewed vigor.

SUPPORTING OUR DAUGHTERS' DREAMS, DAY AND NIGHT

Dreams can also be defined as aspirations, things we hope to
accomplish. During early adolescence our daughters are
filled with all kinds of hopes and dreams. They wonder what
adulthood will bring. They watch the women's soccer team
win the World Cup and imagine themselves on the field.
They watch celebrities on television and imagine that their
lives must be exciting and wonder what it might be like to
actually live that life. At times their dreams are clear and
achievable, but on other days they have no idea what they
want to accomplish, especially when they can't even decide
which outfit to wear. Adolescence is a time of fierce independence coupled with tremendous self-doubt.

How can we show support for our daughters' dreams?
One of the greatest gifts we can give our daughters as they
come of age is to encourage them to dream, to reach for the
stars, and to imagine that anything is possible. Infusing
them with positive energy, creative ideas, and unlimited
thinking inspires them to envision their full potential. We
can support our daughters' dreams by encouraging them to

believe that they can be or do anything they imagine. When my daughter was born, one of our friends gave her a book entitled, *What You Can See, You Can Be.* This is a great message for all of us and is powerful medicine for the self-doubts and negative thoughts that like to hitch a ride on our souls.

There are many well-known people we can look to for inspiration and even proof that "what we can see, we can be," what we can imagine, we can make happen, and that our dreams do come true. Who would have thought that Oprah Winfrey, a poor girl from Arkansas, could become the queen of daytime TV, or that Sally Ride would join the ranks of the male-dominated space industry and become the first female astronaut. Who are the other women you know who have dared to dream?

MOTHER–DAUGHTER ACTIVITY
"I Have a Dream"

Martin Luther King, Jr., was a modern-day dreamer and visionary. Begin a journal entry with the words, "I have a dream," and write nonstop for ten minutes. Allow the words to flow, even if they don't make sense, and then let your own waking dream unfold.

The Modern-Day Dreaming Goddess

The modern-day dreaming goddess is valued for her ability to dream. She invites her dreams to guide and inspire her. She recognizes that her dreams support her intuition, creativity, and aspirations. She welcomes the dream goddess through her prayers and meditations each night as she drifts off to sleep. She dares to dream and knows that what she can see, she can be. She knows that both her nighttime and daytime dreams can reveal the path to her highest potential.

6

Moon Beams

Expressing Your Creativity

●◑○◐●

My friend Lynn graduated with a double major in sociology and cultural anthropology before she went on to study law. She passed the bar without a problem. She worked as an immigration lawyer for many years and though her heart was in her cause, it wasn't in the practice of law. And then one day many years later, she discovered an art form—making tile mosaics. "Now," she tells me, "I have found my passion!" She collects old discarded tiles, dishes, plates, and even coffee mugs and uses these beautiful, colored pieces of ceramic to create vases, tabletops, birdbaths, and garden benches.

"I'd rather walk onto a construction site and ask a bunch of guys for the remains of the demolished kitchen or bathroom than step into a courtroom any day—this is so much more fun!" she exclaimed. "Look what I found last weekend at a yard sale," she continued excitedly as she led me through her work space, a covered patio right off her kitchen that overlooks one of the magnificent green canyons in Santa Barbara. The view is reason enough to inspire a career change, but then she showed me what she had been

"A creative woman is one who follows her passion and finds a way to do what she loves."

Elizabeth Herron,
The Fierce Beauty Club

collecting for her next round of mosaic projects. She had organized buckets of broken tiles, chunks of marble, and funky vintage pieces. She showed me a mirror frame she was getting ready to cover with an assortment of broken ceramic pieces, including one piece from an old mug that depicted the painted face of a young girl.

When I asked her how she got started, Lynn told me about her cousin who makes mosaics, and she said that every time she saw her cousin's collection she secretly wished for a special mosaic-tiled gift. A couple of years ago, right before Christmas, Lynn stumbled into a nursery and saw some mosaic stepping stones. In her own tradition of making homemade gifts for her friends and family, she bought some books and began to experiment. That first Christmas, she made about six mosaic stepping stones, plus a table for her parents, and she continues to learn new techniques and create new pieces. Besides hunting for materials, her favorite part of the process is near the end, when she wipes away the excess grout and can see the beautiful pattern emerge. But what she also really loves is getting messy. As a result Lynn has learned to be so much more understanding of her own daughter's creative mess making. That's how creativity usually is: messy! Her six-year-old daughter, Hannah, likes to work side by side with Lynn and create her own treasures.

"Sometimes, I get so energized when I'm doing this, I could work forever," enthused Lynn. "I want to buy an old used pickup truck so I can haul more of this stuff home, and I'm going to set up a workshop in my garage. Then I'm heading to Mexico so I can find some really great materials—more tiles and some wrought-iron furniture."

"You've lost your logical, lawyer's mind," I teased her. "Though I must say, it sounds like a great plan."

Lynn isn't the only person I know who has begun to reconnect with her creative spirit. My friend Colleen, who has been an artist her whole life, put her talent for graphic art and her passion for improvisational comedy on hold for many years to raise her children and cofound a charter school in Santa Barbara. She has been an administrator there for the past nine years, employing primarily her left brain. She came to one of my writing groups about a year ago, seeking a little nourishment for her creative soul. She immediately began writing poetry again and pretty soon had drafted the first chapter of a novel. It didn't take long for her to discover an untapped well of creative energy and ideas within herself, and in the past year she has created and produced four original board games.

After my friend Laurie's husband, Russ, died, she rekindled her relationship with music and was able to find joy and passion again. While Russ was dying, she kept an altar in a corner of her living room, a sacred space for her candles, goddess figurines, and her and her daughter's prayers. After he died, she took down the altar and moved it into her bedroom, and left the space empty where it had stood. Then one day, as she stood in her living room looking at the empty space, she asked herself, "What do I really love? What really moves me? Where does my passion lie?" She felt an intuitive impulse to fill the corner with all of her musical instruments. In the empty space, Laurie put her flutes, drums, percussion instruments, and an auto harp she had been given by Russ shortly before he died. When her daughter asked her what she was doing, she told her that she felt that it was time to fill that space with music.

Though Laurie had majored in music in college and had sung in the choral society, she gave up her dream opportunity to sing in a jazz band right after she started living with her husband. She was invited to join a jazz trio as well, but chose the relationship instead, and let go of her dream.

The very same day that she had filled the corner of her living room with music, she ran into an old friend and her husband at a local restaurant. Laurie told the couple how she had arranged her musical instruments in the living room. She talked about how she loved to sing. Coincidentally, (or maybe a little goddess synchronicity?), the husband, Willie, happened to need a singer for his band. Laurie has now been singing from her soul for the last four years and filling her heart and her home with music.

These stories remind me of the myth of Hina, the Polynesian moon goddess, who longed to live in a place where she was free to embrace her creative spirit.

The Myth of Hina, The Polynesian Moon Goddess

On the night of the full moon, an image appears on the face of the moon. In the islands of Hawaii, the trade winds tell the story of Hina, the woman who lives in the moon. She is a beautiful goddess with hair as black as night and eyes as shiny as the stars.

Hina did not always live in the moon. Long ago, in old Hawaii, Hina lived in a cave under Rainbow Falls. There she made the best tapa cloths in all of Hawaii. She worked hard to turn plain tree bark into beautiful cloth and decorated it with everything she saw in nature. She borrowed the shapes of leaves and shells and she used the stripes on tropical fish for her designs. Hina's tapa was the best in the land; everyone wanted to wear her cloths. There was always a great demand for her work, but she could not be rushed.

"Tapa is finished when it's ready," Hina would say, "no faster and no slower." Hina made the tapa cloths for her people's finest occasions, and they knew it was worth the wait. It was only her husband who did not appreciate her work. He was a lazy man who complained about everything.

"You are slower than dripping sugar-cane syrup," he said, as he stuffed himself full of fresh coconut, roast pork, and golden ripe bananas, foods that were *kapu*, or forbidden, to Hina because she was a woman.

As much as Hina loved creating beautiful tapa for the village, she was tired of her husband's demands and of being denied the same privileges that men received. Hina dreamed of a place where she would be free to enjoy the pleasures of life in the beautiful world she loved. And she longed for the freedom to make her tapa without having other endless chores to do.

So one day, Hina decided to look for another home and to leave the cave she shared with her husband under Rainbow Falls. She slipped out of her cave one evening while her husband snored loudly and followed a path to the mountaintop. There she prayed to her guardian spirit, Lauhuki, to help her find her new home. She sat quietly gazing into the heavens until the full moon rose above her. She knew her prayer had been answered when she saw the moon-bow, as beautiful as any rainbow, complete with all her favorite colors. Constellations of stars filled the night sky, like tiny diamonds pointing the way to her new home. Hina knew that Lauhuki was guiding her to the moon. She stepped onto the trailing light of a shooting star and was swiftly carried to her new home. When Hina reached the moon's luminous orb, her spirit began to dance freely and she knew that she was finally home.

From that night on, the people of Hawaii have looked to the moon and called her *mahina*, remembering their beloved Hina and the beauty she brought to their world. Whenever the moon is full, the beautiful goddess can be seen sitting with her board and mallet, joyfully making tapa for all to see.

◗○◗

With your daughter, make a cloth similar to Hawaiian tapa. You will need light-colored, 100% cotton muslin, cut to the finished size; mordant or soda ash (found at swimming-pool supply stores); terracotta modeling clay, found in craft stores (a small package will make many finished cloths); and a paintbrush. To create the cloth, you'll need to wash the muslin to remove its sizing. Soak it in water for twenty minutes, with three tablespoons of soda ash per gallon of water. Then remove the muslin, wring out the water, let it dry, and iron the fabric once it has dried. Lightly sketch a design on the muslin. Mix the terracotta clay and some water until you have a thin mixture the texture of paint. Paint the negative space—the space surrounding your design—with this clay-and-water mixture. By painting the negative space, your "design" remains the color of the muslin.

THE GODDESS OF CREATIVITY AND INSPIRATION

It's no wonder that Hina felt more at home on the moon. The moon is a symbol of the divine feminine, and creativity is an essential quality of the feminine soul. Many women today are finding new purpose through their creative passions, as they seek and discover new forms of creative self-expression. Lynn, Colleen, and Laurie have all been successful in their professional roles as lawyer, administrator, and doctor, but their creativity now adds a whole new dimension to their lives.

We all have the power to create, and yet sometimes our creative dreams and passions get buried, lost, or even forgotten. Maybe someone else didn't value them, or we didn't believe in them. Like Hina, we live in a culture that for many years has not placed the same value on artistic expression as it has on other forms of work and achievement.

When we embrace our creative spirits and learn to express ourselves creatively, we feel inspired and alive. Creative and passionate expression is essential to the feminine soul.

Sometimes our creative fires get turned down, burn a little low, and even smolder, but the sparks can be rekindled and ignited. And then new forms of self-expression are born.

Laurie remembered her own creative power and passion when she began to sing and play music again, and now she prescribes passion to her patients. She is a doctor of homeopathy and Chinese medicine and has a thriving family health-care practice in Santa Barbara, where she treats women, men, and children. She takes a mind-body-spirit approach to disease and healing and believes that "health is a radiant state of being, and that a radiant state of being is our true nature and birthright." Laurie knows the medicinal value of passionate, creative, life-force energy. She always asks her patients, "What are your passions? What makes your heart sing? What do you love?" How a patient answers these questions tells Laurie almost everything she needs to know to begin creating a healing process with her patients and to support and assist them in living authentic, passionate, and radiantly healthy lives.

RECLAIMING YOUR CREATIVE SPIRIT

In recent years I have devoured any book I could get my hands on regarding creativity. For me, these books have satisfied a hunger, a craving I'd been experiencing for years: the desire to be creative and to reclaim my creative spirit. In my own family, my sister was always the "creative one." I coveted her art supplies, sketchbooks, colored pencils and pastels, and watercolors. After school I would sit across from her at our round, olive-green kitchen table and watch with envy as she sketched, drew, and painted pictures with a talent I was convinced was not mine. I was in the math and science honors programs and had homework to do. So there we sat, my sister immersed in her art, and me with my nose in a book of equations.

Though most of our activities in this book have been for mothers and daughters to do together, there are times when it's necessary for mothers to indulge themselves alone. This is one of those times. Plan a creative adventure for yourself or spend some quiet moments alone. This is the time to let your imagination wander and to follow your own muse. Indulge yourself!

My creative spirit began to emerge when I came across an old table at a garage sale. I brought it home, painted it a vibrant blue, and used it as a place where my young daughters could be creative. The table was always covered in glue, paint, and glitter. Soon I began to dabble along with my daughters, and I often found myself alone at the table, finishing a project long after they had found other things to keep them busy. Even though my daughters have outgrown that little table, we still try to find time to dabble. Saturday afternoons often find us mucking about at the kitchen table.

I have also made it a priority to find time for creative adventures alone. I like to hang out in places with elements that I love, like fabric stores filled with multicolored, richly woven tapestries, deep, lush velvets, or light and shimmering silks and satins. I also love art stores with their myriad pens and papers, and beaches where I can collect beach glass and shells.

And yet creativity is not always something to rush out and do. Allowing our uncensored inner artist to emerge takes trust, patience, and a willingness to change a few core beliefs. Sitting quietly in your favorite chair and allowing inspiration to find you can be a creative adventure, too.

Calling the Muse: The Nine Muses—Greek Goddesses of Creativity and Inspiration

Mnemosyne, daughter of the Earth Mother, Gaia, birthed nine beautiful and talented daughters who became the Muses, the Greek goddesses of creative inspiration. Though they often visited their father, Zeus, on Mount Olympus, they were raised by their mother on Mount Helicon in ancient Greece. High on the mountaintop, surrounded by nature, Mnemosyne's daughters were free to wander around and their minds were open and keen. Mnemosyne, whose name means "of memory," intended for her daughters to have sharp memories and expansive imaginations of their own.

Mnemosyne knew her daughters would need plenty of time to learn and play. She encouraged them to explore their mountaintop together and made sure that they also had enough quiet time alone for solitary reverie. They took turns gallivanting on their beloved winged horse, Pegasus, and they frolicked in the mountain's streams and meadows. They drank from the geysers that sprang up from beneath Pegasus's hooves and were refreshed with Gaia's effervescent waters. Later, they sat quietly beneath her shady trees.

Mnemosyne wanted her daughters to appreciate culture and the art of natural beauty. She was a gifted teacher and taught her daughters to attune their senses to nature, where they learned to hear and channel sound and rhythm. They learned to see with heightened awareness and hold images in their mind's eye. Most importantly, Mnemosyne encouraged her daughters to muse, resulting in their highly developed memories and imaginations.

As her daughters grew, their unique gifts and individual talents emerged, easily distinguishing them from one another. Calliope was the oldest of the sisters. She is the muse of epic poetry and storytelling and inspires all forms of poetry. Clio is the muse of history and writing and also inspires journal, let-ter, and autobiographical writing. Erato, who awakens and brings love into the world, is the muse of love poetry. Euterpe is the muse of music and inspires song, sound, and music of all kinds. Melpomene is the muse of tragedy and inspires the expression of grief. She is referred to as the songstress of suf-fering, sorrow, and sweet laments. Polyhymnia is the muse of hymns, spoken words, and sacred poetry. Terpsichore, mean-ing "she who loves to dance," is the muse of dance and reminds us that the body is a creative instrument. Thalia, the muse of comedy, brings us joy, laughter, and a sense of play.

She enjoys mischief and all kinds of revelry. Urania, the muse of astronomy and science, inspires discovery, invention, and original thought. She stirs the imagination and creative impulse of the scientist and inventor.

Mnemosyne raised her daughters well. She ignited the spark of their creative spirit, which since antiquity they have passed on to all mortals who have sought their divine inspiration.

◐○○

COME DANCE WITH ME

My daughter Austin, like many young girls, was a classic tomboy throughout elementary school, and dressed the part right down to her skateboarding shoes. Jeans, T-shirts, and cargo pants were her signature fashion style for years. She loved and participated in sports of all kinds, including coed roller hockey and flag football. I admired her independent spirit and her ability to easily cross gender lines. Except for the ballet class she had taken when she was five years old, she had never shown an interest in dance.

"The best part was the cookie you brought me afterwards from that coffee place next door," she told me when I asked her several years later what she remembered about that ballet class, and if she had any more interest in dance.

Several of her friends had been involved in a fabulous jazz-dance program directed and taught by Steven, a teacher who is so inspiring, fun-loving, and cool, I'd love to be a kid in one of his classes.

When Austin was in the fifth grade, I got a call from my friend Kimberly, who wanted to know if I thought Austin might like to take one of Steven's jazz classes with her daughter Natalie.

"Kimberly, there's just no way Austin is going to take a jazz class," I resolutely informed her. "But in all fairness, I'll go ask her." I headed for her room to make the cursory inquiry, already imagining the face I was sure she would make at me.

"Hey, Austin, how would you like to take a jazz-dance class with Natalie?"

"Sure, I'll try it," she responded, without the face.

Floored, I staggered back to the telephone, smart enough to accept her simple and concise answer without any further questions. The next week, Austin put on a pair of black jazz pants and lace-up jazz shoes and started the class with her friend Natalie. Even when Natalie had to drop the class, Austin stayed with it, dancing twice a week and performing in seasonal dance recitals for two more years, loving every minute of it. One day I confessed to her that I had been surprised and delighted when she said yes to the class.

"You hated that creative ballet class you took when you were five," I reasoned.

"Mom, I had to wear a tutu, okay, and don't even remind me of that!"

When Austin started dancing she connected with a part of herself that she had not known before. Through Steven's jazz program Austin discovered music and dancing, which added a new dimension to her life. Dancing offered her a new way to express herself, and the experience was transformative. In fact, at the end of the school year, she wrote an essay declaring Steven the most influential person in her life that year. The next year, she got one of the female leads in her class play, The Music Man. The following summer, she was singing her first solo on stage at the final performance put on by her summer theater camp.

"OH, FIDDLESTICKS"

Emma, my thirteen-year-old daughter, has been playing the violin for several years. I had always thought of the violin in classical terms—orchestras, virtuosos, and the like. But what Emma has been drawn to is fiddling. Folk songs, bluegrass, and Appalachian tunes are what she plays now. She and her teacher play together each week at her lesson, with her teacher most often accompanying her on the guitar. Emma has played with other adults and kid musicians around the campfire at our annual homeschooling campouts. She has found confidence and creativity by sharing her music with others.

Austin and Emma have discovered ways in which to express their creativity, often in ways that surprised me. It is quite likely that they will be drawn to other Muses as they continue to discover their passions.

Dancer, choreographer, and teacher Martha Graham once said, "There is a vitality, a life force, an energy, a quickening that is translated through you into action, and because there is only one of you in all time, this expression is unique. And if you block it, it will never exist through any other medium and be lost, the world will not have it."

Our role is to help our daughters keep their creative channels open and their creative power and energy alive.

WHAT A MESS—IF MARTHA STEWART COULD SEE US NOW

Last Thanksgiving, my daughters and I had four days to be together without school, schedules, or homework, to just hang out and do nothing. I must admit, in the past I would sometimes dread these long, continuous days without a break. Over time I've learned how to spend endless hours in the giving role while refilling my own cup at the same time. I've discovered that creativity is a resource as well as a way to re-source.

Late in the morning on Friday, after we'd had plenty of time to lounge around in our pajamas, we gathered in the kitchen and turned it into a chaotic and messy hub of creativity. First, Austin and I made a pie—she made the crust and I made the filling. Together we transformed our last uncarved pumpkin into a hearty and tasty dessert. Fresh pumpkin and molasses, I would have never guessed, is divine.

With the pie in the oven, Austin headed into cyberspace and it was Sarah's turn to make a mess. With her friend McKensey, we opened the art closet, a completely random and haphazard avalanche waiting to happen, and hauled out the bag of fabric scraps, recycled tissue paper, leftover ends of yarn, and last summer's saved (and washed) Popsicle sticks. We spent the next couple of hours making angels. Nothing fancy—sort of like the pie, a little of this and that—we made them by using whatever we had in the house. Cotton balls formed the angels' heads, fabric made the dress, and tissue paper became the wings.

As she was gluing the tiny glass beads on the face of her angel, McKensey looked up and smelled the warm, mingling scent of cinnamon, nutmeg, butter, and flour, and commented, "This is sort of like a Martha Stewart day."

"Yeah," I laughed, "only a lot messier." The floor was covered with flour, pie crust, fabric scraps, and pieces of yarn. I looked around the kitchen, which usually embarrasses me with its white floor I can never keep clean, and for the first time I appreciated the dirt and the clutter. Creativity can be pretty messy, but it's also delicious, fun, warm, and cozy, especially on a cold November day.

What I've learned about the creative process is that creativity is messy, random, and chaotic. It is anything but neat, tidy, logical, or linear, though I'm sure it could be enhanced by a good dose of feng shui—the art of placement. To support our daughters' creative explorations, as mothers we have to be prepared to let go, allow the messes to happen, and let our daughters choose their own ways of expression. Like Lynn's mosaic pieces, we need to trust that at some point, divine creation will emerge from under the cloudy, messy gray grout.

MOTHER–DAUGHTER ACTIVITY
Ignite Your Creative Spirit

Make a treasure-filled candle with your daughter. You will need a candle container, wax, wicks, wick clips, fragrance, color, and an assortment of small trinkets and treasures. Heat the wax in a pan over low heat until it turns to liquid. Add the fragrance, color, and trinkets to the wax. Measure the wick to the candle height, plus half an inch. Put the wick holder on the end of the wick and place it in the center of the container. Pour the wax into the container, keeping the wick in the center. Let the candle set for forty-eight hours. Take off the container and trim the wick. Light the candle and watch your treasures emerge.

IGNITE YOUR CREATIVE SPIRIT

One Christmas vacation, my daughter's stepmother taught them how to make candles, and I was the lucky recipient of one of these beautiful and fragrant gifts. When I lit the wick, the light blue- and violet-colored wax slowly melted down to reveal an abundance of hidden treasures, such as little trinkets, charms, and beads. And each time I lit the candle, a new gift would emerge from its core. We are all like these candles, in that deep within us are our own hidden treasures, our creative gifts and passions, waiting to be revealed. Some of these gifts are closer to the surface, more obvious and easier to see, and others are more deeply buried and require time, patience, and trust to coax out.

Help you daughter ignite her own creative spirit and then watch her gifts emerge.

The Modern-Day Hina

Today's Hina is free to embrace her creative spirit. Inspired by her own inner muses, she explores different ways to express her creative passions and likes to spend quiet moments with her imagination. She knows that her creativity is the vital life-force energy that is connected to her spirit. She confidently reveals her creative gifts and celebrates the unique expression of her soul.

7
Moon Reflection
Honoring Your Body

●○◐○●

"Mommy, do you ever think about being thinner?" my ten-year-old daughter asked from the back seat of the car one morning on our way to school. Once I got past my initial thought that perhaps she was suggesting that I should lose some weight, I realized that I had been given a golden opportunity, plus a (literally) captive audience in my car. This is the main reason I don't mind the fifteen-minute drive to and from school each day: some of our best conversations happen in my red Toyota. For the last six months Sarah, had been increasingly critical of her own body, even using the F word (fat) to describe it. "So how honest am I willing to be?" I wondered in the few moments I had to formulate an appropriate response to her question. Did I want to tell her that being thin had been an obsession of mine for most of my life? Should I mention all of the unhealthy ways in which I had sought to achieve a culturally ideal body image, that is until I turned forty and began my new quest for self-acceptance?

"Yes, I do think about being thinner," I confessed. "But these days, I am much more interested in accepting myself

"To lose confidence in one's body is to lose confidence in oneself."

Simone de Beauvoir

and my body the way I am. My body is strong and healthy and I'm grateful for that." And here's my favorite part: "I am a goddess," I told her. "And so are you." I like to say that from time to time, in case I begin to forget again.

"That's good, Mommy. I like that," she replied, then hugged me and climbed out of the car.

I watched her walk into the schoolyard, marveling at how strong, sturdy, and well-proportioned her body is, and acknowledging how tender and vulnerable she also is on the inside. I felt like I'd been able to plant one small seed in her very fertile and receptive mind, and I knew that she was just beginning to face the inevitable challenge of being a female in a culture that has forgotten that the female body is to be revered and celebrated, and that true beauty comes from within. I drove away wondering how I could help my daughter learn to accept and even love the natural body she has been graced with, and to discover and celebrate her true inner beauty.

I have been vigilant about not bringing negative body- and weight-related topics into our household. We do not own a scale, count calories, diet, or talk about our weight or fat. In spite of my best efforts, I know that the culture we live in makes it nearly impossible for girls and women to appreciate and accept their bodies. Studies show that over half of all girls are unhappy with their bodies by the age of thirteen. We are constantly bombarded with unattainable images and definitions of physical beauty. Most advertisements are computer-enhanced and airbrushed to produce a culturally idealistic and physically unrealistic female form. Not even the women in those advertisements look like they do in the final copy. The truth is, actresses and models wake up just like we do, with blemishes and insecurities about their physical appearance.

In a recent interview, actress Gwyneth Paltrow confessed her own insecurities about her body. "Sure I'm insecure," she admitted. "I never think that I'm thin enough or my boobs are big enough or whatever." She blamed the media for pressuring women to be thin. "We are bombarded with images of twelve-year-old girls with makeup and we think we are supposed to look like that. Well, I'm never gonna look like me either," she continued. "With the way they airbrush the pictures and all, I don't look like that." (*Santa Barbara News Press*, November 9, 2001).

A couple of days later, I decided to check on the seed I'd planted in the back seat of my Toyota to find out if it was germinating, or if it had been blown away by the wind. I was in the car again with my daughter, this time driving home.

"So what would you do," I asked her, "if you were a mother and you had a beautiful and precious little girl who thought she was too fat?"

"And you mean she wasn't?" she asked.

"Yeah," I continued. "What would you tell her or want her to know about her body?"

She was quiet for a moment, then replied, "Well, the most important thing is that she not criticize it. And I'd want her to know that she was beautiful however she was."

Maybe I had found a fellow passenger on my journey toward self-acceptance. As I turned the corner, I wondered, "Where do we go from here?"

Once again, we must turn to the goddess.

"The body is a sacred garment. It's your first and last garment; it is what you enter life in and what you depart life with, and it should be treated with honor."
—Martha Graham

THE GREAT EARTH GODDESSES

The mysterious power of the female body has been expressed in art, religion, and mythology since the beginning of time. The earliest humans living on earth observed the magical and synchronistic correlations between the earth and women's bodies. Mythology from every culture in the world deify the earth as the Great Goddess and celebrate her ability to create and sustain life. One of the oldest creation myths and first names given to the Great Goddess is Gaia. Gaia is the ancient Earth Mother, a metaphor for the female body. The myths and images of the Great Goddess as a full and powerful female offer women and girls a natural understanding and perhaps a new perspective of our female bodies. What if our daughters could see the correlation between their own female bodies and that of Gaia, the Great Goddess, the earth? What if our daughters could re-imagine their own female bodies to be goddesslike?

The Myth of Gaia

Spinning, spiraling, dancing freely, Gaia rolled herself out of the vast and timeless universe into an earthy ball. She sculpted from her soft, brown form majestic mountains, rounded hills, flat plains, and deep valleys, and she filled her crevasses with oceans and streams of water. The sun kissed her exquisite body, bringing forth strong and sturdy trees, medicinal and edible plants, and beautiful and fragrant flowers. The heavenly sky rained upon her, bathing her with a warm and gentle shower. Soon Gaia was covered with a rainbow of sparkling colors—turquoise and sapphire blues, emerald greens and ruby reds—and jewels adorned her flesh. Gaia was filled with joy, and a creative life-force energy pulsated through her body and radiated from her being. She continued to spin in a cosmic ecstasy and she celebrated her new life and form. Gaia loved her new fullness, with all of its curves and contours, and wanted to share with other energies and spirits the joy of living in a body.

In time, her fertile earth body conceived of other living creations in many colors, shapes, and forms. Gaia, the Great Mother and earth goddess, loved and cared for them all. She nourished them with an abundance of flora and fauna and refreshed them with clear, cool waters. Blessed by the sun and with her sister, the moon, Gaia created a harmonious rhythm of cycles and seasons, and all of her creatures danced around her in a joyous circle of life.

The creation myth of Gaia illuminates the correlation between the earth body, with her rolling hills, river valleys, and natural contours and waters, and our own natural bodies. The idea of the earth as a metaphor for the female body is not a new concept. Goddess images—statues, figurines, drawings, carvings, and sculptures—from all over the world portray the female body as full and abundant and celebrate the body's power to create and sustain life.

◐○○

MOTHER–DAUGHTER ACTIVITY
Goddess Art and Body Talk

Choose a goddess-related art book from the library or bookstore. *Goddesses in Art*, by Lanier Graham, and *The Heart of the Goddess—Art, Myth, and Meditations of the World's Sacred Feminine*, by Hallie Austen Iglehart, are just two of the many wonderful resources containing images of goddesses in sculpture, paintings, and photographs. Look at these images with your daughter and share your impressions of these different works of art. Then select some current fashion magazines and look at those pictures of women. Ask her: *"How would you describe the body types of these models?" "Are there any other variations?" "How representative of current culture are these models' bodies?" "How realistic do you think these bodies are?" "What would it take to create a body of this type?" "What would be the purpose of working to create this particular body type?"* Compare these photographs with the images you saw in the goddess books, then create your own description of a beautiful body, remembering the goddess Gaia and the ancient reverence for the female body.

THE POWER OF ACCEPTANCE—TRUE BEAUTY IS AN INSIDE JOB

Because Austin inherited her father's body type, which is tall and thin, I can't use the argument with Sarah (who got my shorter, fuller frame) that thin is unnatural. The truth is that bodies come in all shapes and sizes. Since Sarah and Austin were infants, they've grown differently. Austin was thin even as a baby, though she ate well. Sarah, born about three years later, was round and sturdy. As young children, they ate the same food and went to the park and rode bikes together, but their bodies remained completely different. There are times when Austin frets about her thinness and times when Sarah worries that she is fat, but the conversation in our house continues to be about body types and self-acceptance. There is not one universal body type!

Sixteen-year-old Mikaila and four of her friends share clothes so often that I no longer know which clothes are actually hers. She has the wardrobe of five for the price of one—not a bad deal! The girls range in height from 5'3" to 5'9" and weigh from about 100 to 120 pounds. None of them have the same body size or shape and not one of them looks like those emaciated models who appear on the covers of fashion magazines, yet they are all healthy, fit, and a slim size three or five. Of course, sometimes pants need to be pinned up and some waists sag, but by conventional standards they are all the same size. As they mature, their bodies will settle into a natural shape unique to each girl. I sometimes see them pat their stomachs and moan about imagined rolls of fat or eye themselves in the mirror and fret about their derrières, but for the most part they are content to be who they are. They appreciate each other for things other than the way they look. They are not just beautiful teenagers, but budding actresses, artists, athletes, and singers. They may not be able to share clothes for the rest of their lives, but their power is in the acceptance of their uniqueness.

As mothers we can set an example of self-acceptance by not worrying and fretting about our own weight and appearance, but rather by focusing on a healthy lifestyle with good food and plenty of exercise. We can acknowledge our daughters' outer beauty while continuing to remind them of their inner beauty. The reasons we love them are not their long curly hair, those baby-blue or chocolate-brown eyes, or those cute little figures, but because they are our daughters—warm, funny, smart, sensitive, and much more. We love who they are, not just how they look, and we say that to them over and over again.

Sometimes guided visualizations help us absorb and assimilate new ideas on a deeper level. Using a taped visualization or the one in the activity on page 94, guide your daughter through a visualization exercise. (All it takes is about ten minutes.) Focus on something different about your body each time—radiant skin, standing tall, and feeling confident. Visualize strong and powerful legs that kick the winning goal.

"Living in a woman's body is not easy," writes Geneen Roth in her book *Breaking Free from Compulsive Eating*. "Especially if you happen to look like a woman and not like an adolescent boy. We've spent years trying to slice away what makes our bodies womanly: the roundness, the lushness. And we've sliced our spirits instead. We've listened for so long to what they—our parents, our doctors, our lovers, our fashion moguls, our Hollywood directors—decide is attractive that we've lost our own voices. We don't know who we are anymore. And we can't wait any longer for them to tell us. We can't wait until they decide that it's acceptable for a woman to look like a woman. We can't wait until they give us permission to enjoy our bodies, until they tell

MOTHER–DAUGHTER ACTIVITY
Body Sculpt

Get yourself some earthy brown or gray clay. If that's too messy, you can also use modeling clay or beeswax. With your daughter, create your own images of an earth goddess. If you feel bold, sculpt an image of your own physical body, and treat it with loving care! Feel the power of your feminine spirit.

Have a spa day with your daughter. Facials, manicures, and pedicures are great ways to nourish and care for our bodies. There are many books and magazine articles that describe beauty treatments using ingredients that can be found in your kitchen. Create cornmeal scrubs, oatmeal masks, and minty steams. You can also treat yourselves to a professional experience. How about a massage?

us it's possible that some women are meant to be larger than others. They might be afraid of bodies that bleed, create, and sustain life. They might always be afraid of women who are unafraid. We can't wait until all the people who fear passionate, powerful women get in touch with those fears instead of projecting them and turning women into sex objects. Their work is to own the fears; our work is to own our power."

Encourage your daughter to look in a full-length mirror and imagine an aura of power around her. Do the body sculpting activity on page 95 remembering that image.

BEYOND ACCEPTANCE: HONORING AND CELEBRATING OUR BODIES

Sarah, my ten-year-old, has always loved art. At a young age she began to dabble in mixed media, and her body was often her canvas. When she was three years old, she rubbed Elmer's glue on her bare belly and sprinkled it with sparkling flecks of gold glitter. When I brought out the brown earthy clay, she rubbed that too onto her belly, face, arms, and legs. And naturally, when the watercolors came out later on, her body became her canvas again. When she was six years old, she wore purple, blue, and green eye shadow, her fingernails sparkled with multicolored polish, and she wore "guava frost" lipstick. Today, she wears shiny lip gloss, colored nail polish, and body glitter on her cheeks and eyelids. She has braved the ear gun at a local jewelry store and has multiple piercings in her ears. She hopes to someday pierce her belly button.

There is a natural instinct to beautify, adorn, and celebrate the female body. Body adornment and beautification practices have existed in many cultures since the beginning of time, and the practice has been used for social and spiritual, as well as beautification, purposes.

Our most current and popular body art and adornment rituals include wearing jewelry, applying makeup, hair coloring and perming, head shaving, nail polishing, tattooing, and piercing. What are some other self-loving and self-caring body practices we can teach to and share with our daughters? How about a spa day?

The Modern-Day Gaia

The modern-day Gaia accepts the uniqueness of her own earth body and revels in its power. Through adornment and self-loving care, she honors and celebrates the sacredness of her body. Today's Gaia knows that true beauty comes from within. From her radiant core she lets her light shine.

8

Moon Time
Celebrating Menstruation

●○○●●

"How might it have been different for you," asks Judith Duerk, "if, on your first menstrual day, your mother had given you a bouquet of flowers and taken you to lunch, and then the two of you had gone to meet your father at the jeweler, where your ears were pierced, and your father bought you your first pair of earrings, and then you went with a few of your friends and your mother's friends to get your first lip coloring, and then you went, for the very first time, to the Women's Lodge, to learn the wisdom of the women? How might your life be different?"

The first time I read this passage in *Circle of Stones—Woman's Journey to Herself*, I thought about my own first period, which for me was mostly characterized by the absence of event. Even though I had secretly looked forward to it, once it began the magic was over, and it became simply something that got in my way each month, especially when I was on the high-school swim team. Later, I prayed for my period as a sign that I wasn't pregnant, and when I wanted to become pregnant, I prayed that it would not come. It wasn't until my youngest daughter was

"What happens at a girl's first menstruation is very important and can affect her for years to come, influencing how she feels about her periods, her sexuality, her womanhood."

Dena Taylor, *Red Flower— Rethinking Menstruation*

Just for Mothers

What do you remember about your first period? What kinds of messages and information did you receive before your first period started? How did you feel and how were you treated when your first period began? How do you view your menstrual cycle today? Reflect on how these first experiences influenced you and think about the message you would like your daughter to receive.

a year old and I had been nursing or pregnant for almost five years that I really noticed my cycles—by their absence. I missed the way I had experienced a monthly rhythm, even the highs and the lows, and could feel something powerful cycling through me. For the first time since I was thirteen years old, I wanted to start my period again. I remember, in fact, the morning I said a prayer to the moon.

On a family vacation to the south shore of Kauai, I woke up early one morning and slipped out just after sunrise for a solitary walk on the beach and to collect some fresh plumeria and hibiscus blossoms. The moon had been full the night before and the tide was quite low. I walked out on a sandbar to face the sunrise and when I looked behind me, I saw the faint yet full moon still lingering in the sky. I was so surprised to see it there, I must have jumped with a start. The moon's unexpected presence felt like a reminder and an invitation, and I remember saying, "Yes, I want you back in my life." I stood there between the rising sun and the setting moon and asked the moon to restore my menstrual cycle. After a few moments, I walked slowly back to the house, carrying a hope and a promise and a handful of red and yellow flowers. Three months later, my cycle returned. It had taken me more than twenty years to appreciate the value of my menstrual cycle.

Though it's too late to change the circumstances of our own first periods, it's not too late to change our perspective on menstruation so that we can make the menstrual experience different for our daughters.

The Myth of Hera, Goddess of the New Moon

When the sun rose on the ancient Greek village of Argos, Elena gently woke her mother and her older sister. Her grandmother was already awake and was putting a few special things into her straw basket.

"Congratulations, dear one. Today you will have your first bath at Kanathos."

Elena had waited a long time for this day. Each month she had had to watch her mother and grandmother, and recently her older sister, joyfully fill their baskets with their favorite foods, soft blankets, light linens, and moon oil, and leave her behind for the day. She had longed for the time when she, too, would align with Hera, goddess of the new moon, and flow with the other women.

Every morning on the day of the new moon, the women in Elena's family and those of the neighboring huts would leave their village together and walk to the spring of freeing waters to take their ritual bath of renewal and to enjoy a day of rest. They bathed with fragrant herbs and flowers, washed each other's hair, and dried their olive-brown skin in the sun. Then they gathered branches from the Lygos bushes and spread the leaves out in a circle. The Lygos leaves brought forth their sacred blood, cleansing their wombs. The women of Argos menstruated together in synchronicity with the new moon and each month honored this special day with ritual and reverie. They spent the day in quiet conversation, speaking softly to each other so as to not disturb the meditations and visions of the dreamers. Later, they listened to the stories of the elders, always wise, full of knowledge, and spiced with humor. Elena never tired of her grandmother's storytelling and on this special evening, she felt as though she heard every story for the first time.

When the sun began to set and dusk became darkness, the women filled the night with soft singing and low chanting around a fire. The sound of their voices, like a melodious prayer, seemed to call down the moon, and Hera appeared above them as a pale sliver of light. She gave her blessings each month to the women of Argos and bestowed them with fertility of womb and field. As her sacred blood flowed from her maiden's womb, Elena knew that this was the night that she would receive Hera's blessing. Sitting there between her mother and sister with the other women from her mother's clan, she looked into the night sky and understood the infiniteness of her matrilineal line. She smiled up at her divine mother, received her blessing, and felt like a true goddess for the first time.

◗○◖

SACRED MENSTRUATION

The goddess Hera offers ancient wisdom that can give us a new perspective on menstruation. In ancient myth she appears to the women of Argos as they gather together to celebrate menstruation. In ancient times and before the advent of electricity, women's menstrual cycles were synchronized with each other's and with the new moon. Their changing moods, emotions, and energy levels were understood as they were reflected in the changing face of the moon. It was known that the different stages of the moon and menstrual cycles brought different opportunities. Men and women alike viewed menstruation as a sacred, spiritual experience and recognized the enhanced intuition and even visionary abilities that women experienced during it. Women retreated to moon huts, lodges, and tents for the duration of their cycles, and they returned from their quiet gatherings feeling restored, renewed, and re-inspired for the tasks and purposes of their lives.

Today, feelings about menstruation can be confusing. How many women look forward to or celebrate their periods? How many people—men or women—see menstruation as a blessing rather than "the curse"? Five thousand years ago, the female body was revered and honored. Menstruation was sacred because it meant that life would continue. But many women today have negative feelings about menstruation and don't know why. We have inherited and internalized negative attitudes and beliefs about our bodies and menstrual cycles, and legacies of embarrassment and indifference have been passed down from mother to daughter. Besides the box of sanitary pads we were given and the cursory film on menstruation we had to watch, we didn't get much information about menstruation, especially about the deeper wisdom of our cycles.

A goddess perspective gives us a positive and powerful way to share the experience of menstruation and feminine cycles with our daughters.

MOON DAUGHTER—UNDERSTANDING HER MOON CYCLE

Correlating the menstrual cycle with the moon cycle is a great way to explain the natural monthly rhythms and cycles to our daughters. With the moon as a visible mirror,

---

MOTHER–DAUGHTER ACTIVITY
Energy Cycles

The following message was found on an insert in a 1963 tampon box.

WHEN YOU'RE A WIFE*:
Don't take advantage of your husband. That's an old rule of good marriage that's just as sensible now as it ever was. Of course you'll try not to take advantage, but sometimes ways of taking advantage aren't obvious. You *wouldn't connect it with menstruation, for instance. Yet, if you neglect the simple rules that make menstruation a normal time of month, and retire for a few days each month as though you were ill, you're taking advantage of your husband's good nature. He married a full-time wife, not a part-time one. So you should be active, peppy, and cheerful everyday.*

Share this with your daughter and discuss with her the misconceptions and false assumptions about menstruation and the lack of awareness of women's energy cycles. What does this tell you about the pre-vailing beliefs and values of that time?

(*from *Women's Bodies, Women's Wisdom* by Christiane Northrup, M.D.)

a young woman can better understand her own inner cycles, natural rhythms, and experiences.

The moon reflects the ebb and flow of our menstrual cycle. The dark new moon coincides with the time of bleeding and the bright full moon corresponds with ovulation, so the waxing and waning light mirrors our changing energy patterns. The female monthly cycle, like the full cycle of the moon, occurs over a period of about twenty-nine days. Though cycles vary from woman to woman, and though it can take years for a girl's cycles to become regular and consistent, the moon is nonetheless a beautiful reflection of our natural rhythms.

MENARCHE — FIRST MOON

The word *menarche* (pronounced men-ar-key) literally means "beginning" and "moon," and therefore, "first moon," or first period. Perhaps the most important question for a modern-day mother is how to celebrate a daughter's first period.

Menarche and other coming-of-age ceremonies around the world are as diverse as the cultures that perform them. Some of the most beautiful and elaborate menarche ceremonies are performed in India, by Native Americans in the Apache and Navajo tribes, and by the Pygmies in Africa, and are described by Dena Taylor in *Red Flower — Rethinking Menstruation*. The Mescalero Apache girls' puberty ceremony is an annual event celebrating the menarche of all the girls who started their periods in the past year, and includes feasting, gift-giving, and dancing. "It is the most important ceremony of these people," states Taylor, "and they believe that it insures their survival."

One of my favorite descriptions is the menarche rite of passage practiced by the Pygmies in central Africa. "To the Pygmies," claims Taylor, "menstrual blood is a gift, gratefully and joyously received by the entire community. The girl who has reached menarche goes into seclusion in the *elima* house, taking all her young friends with her, where an older female relative teaches them the arts and crafts of motherhood. This is followed by a celebration that lasts a month or two, and friends come from near and far to pay their respects." I love that she takes her friends with her and that they are taught by a woman about womanhood and motherhood.

As our daughters approach and experience their own first moon, we have an opportunity to change the prevailing beliefs about menstruation by changing the way we talk to and treat them at this sacred time. Though many modern girls would probably prefer that their first periods not be publicly celebrated, they can still be honored and celebrated with love and respect.

My daughter Austin can't wait for her first-moon kit. She is even willing to have a first-moon celebration, something I wouldn't have ever thought possible. Austin and I have been talking about these ideas for awhile and as menarche approaches, she is looking at it as something to honor rather than something to hide. She is excited about crossing this threshold into womanhood. "I want to drink red wine out of a wooden bowl when I start my period," she informed me. I was amazed at her unconscious awareness of the powerful metaphor she was describing. A bowl or basket has long been used ceremonially to symbolize the womb, and of course the red wine represents blood.

"I'll prepare a goddess feast and invite a few friends. We'll bring presents, light candles, and pass the wooden bowl of wine," I promised.

HONORING OUR CYCLES

When Mikaila was eleven years old, she crawled into bed with me one cold January morning—something she hadn't done in a long time. She leaned her head on my shoulder and began to cry. Quietly, she told me that she had started her period that morning. I was not surprised; she had shown the first signs of puberty at age nine. Still, she was young and none of her friends had begun to menstruate yet—in fact, many of them were only just beginning puberty. I hugged her and told her it was something to celebrate and that I wanted to honor her and this special rite of passage. I asked her what she might like to do. We spent the afternoon shopping and I bought her a new outfit and a pair of earrings. I suggested that we also buy something that she could keep to remind her of this important passage. She picked out a whimsical pâpier-maché moon fairy and hung it in her window. Five years later, the fairy has survived changing decorating tastes, wall colors, and new furniture and is still hanging in her window. That night we had dinner with another mother and daughter at a fancy restaurant and quietly toasted the occasion and celebrated with good food and friendship.

On the other end of the spectrum is Mikaila's friend Joya. Shortly after Joya turned thirteen, she had a beautiful coming-of-age ceremony that included fifty guests. We gathered in her backyard one sunny spring day and honored her with recollections, gifts, and heartfelt wishes to carry her on her journey into womanhood. Joya loved her celebration. Two years later, the start of Joya's period was a very low-key event with little fanfare. Most of her friends had already been menstruating for some time and Joya had firsthand knowledge of cramps, pads, and teenage menstrual woes. Joya, in fact, refers to the time before her menses began as a "period-free blessing." Like Joya, some girls will not feel the need to celebrate menstruation, but there are still many opportunities and ways to celebrate our daughters as they come of age.

ANGELIKA'S FIRST-MOON CELEBRATION

The invitation that arrived in the mail addressed to Emma and me contained a dark-red card that said:

> *River she is flowing, growing*
> *River she is flowing to the sea.*
> *Carry me to my mother*
> *Your child I will always be*
> *Carry me my mother to the sea*
> *River she is flowing ...*

Inside it read: *"Join us for Angelika Dawn's First-Moon Celebration!"*

There were eight of us—four mothers and four daughters—gathered around an altar of flowers, baby pictures, baby shoes, rocks, shells, and three candles, two white and one red. Angelika wore a crown of flowers made by her friend Luisa. Angelika's mother, Shirley, lit sage and welcomed the wisdom of the four directions. She welcomed us as important women and friends in Angelika's life. We joined hands and each took a turn speaking of our matriarchal lineage. "I am the granddaughter of Grace and Rose, the daughter of Agnes; I am Terri, the sister of Michelle and Amy; I am the mother of Mikaila and Emma." Slowly we were surrounded by the spirit of women, both past and present. We sang, our voices joining together in the simple harmony of friendship.

Angelika's first gift was a spiral-wombed goddess figurine of the earth and sky. Each mother held it as we remembered our own first moons. Our memories were filled with wonder, nostalgia, and laughter. Then our daughters talked about the expectations they had of their own first moon. They spoke of women they admired and described the qualities that made these women important to them.

MOTHER–DAUGHTER ACTIVITY
First-Moon Celebration

Mikaila's and Angelika's first-moon celebrations were very different. The celebrations honored each girl in the way she felt most comfortable. Plan to celebrate your daughter's first moon in a way that feels right for both of you.

Shirley placed a threshold of red ribbon on the floor with candles at both ends. Surrounded on one side by her nonmenstruating friends, Angelika crossed the threshold alone to be welcomed by those of us who had crossed before her. Shirley welcomed her with a taste of honey for the sweet times in her life, a taste of salt for the times that were bitter, and then a bite of strawberry to remind her that the good times always return. Angelika drank raspberry juice as a symbol of the red wine of life. Her mother placed a necklace of garnets and special stones around her neck in honor of her first moon. When we returned to our circle, Angelika received more gifts, including a carved stone mermaid that came apart to reveal hidden compartments containing a red bead, a journal to record her dreams, and a mirror to reflect her inner beauty. We each gave Angelika a river rock that we had inscribed with the things we wished for her—peacefulness, generosity, friendship, intuition, uniqueness, and love—and placed them on the altar. We offered her our blessings and as Luisa put her stone on the altar, she wisely observed, "You can never have enough love."

The Modern-Day Hera

Today's Hera understands the correlation between the monthly cycles of the moon and her own "moon cycles." She honors and appreciates each phase of her own moon time and the changing opportunities offered throughout each cycle. She knows that menarche is a powerful passage to a new stage of her life. She welcomes her first moon with celebration.

9

Moon Love
Discovering Intimacy and Sexuality

●◐○○●

My daughter Austin came home from school last week with a permission slip for me to sign. It said, "It is time in seventh grade when students participate in the Puberty and Human Reproduction unit of health science. This is an important unit because there are so many myths around sexuality from the media and peers that it is crucial for students to have a safe place to learn the facts. I have included a calendar of topics to be presented and discussed." I quickly scanned the calendar: Sexually transmitted infections, pregnancy, birth control, nocturnal emission, spontaneous erections, oral/anal sex, and more. Though Austin has known in detail how babies are made since I was pregnant with her younger sister, and though we talk openly about whatever sexual issues come up, somehow a classroom full of seventh-grade boys and girls didn't exactly feel like a safe place to learn for the first time about a few of the topics listed on the calendar. I appreciated the heads-up, signed the permission slip, and decided I needed to expand her knowledge before the classes began.

"Intimate relationships of all kinds take time and commitment. They take trust. And there's no more intimate relationship than sex."

Joan Borysenko, *A Woman's Journey to God*

I asked Austin which topics she was familiar with and if there was anything she didn't know, and from there I filled in the gaps. Still, it all seemed so flat, dry, and clinical without a frame of reference. Not that I wanted her to have a frame of reference, and these were hardly clinical topics—at least the ones we were talking about. Then I had an idea. She had been asking me ever since her best friend in fifth grade saw the movie *American Pie* if she could see it, too, and for two years I'd been repeatedly saying no. I had already seen it and I knew it was the story of teenage boys on a quest to have sex for the first time, and that it was filled with every sexual reference imaginable, along with several outrageous sexual scenes.

"When, then?" she'd ask, and I just kept hoping it would go away. Well, these topics and issues don't go away, and I felt a strong responsibility to make sure that she was safely and comfortably informed. So, prompted by the seventh-grade Puberty and Human Reproduction unit, I decided that perhaps the movie did have some educational value, and that the time had come for my daughter and me to watch the movie together.

The day before we planned to watch it, I began to have second thoughts. "What does this have to do with the goddess and sacred sexuality?" I asked myself. "This isn't what I want her to know and to accept as normal, appropriate behavior." And yet this movie is a slice of American pie (pun intended), and in many cases representative of what goes on in our culture today. I reminded myself that my job is to make sure she is informed, prepared, and knows what her choices are.

And so on Thursday night, Austin and I sat on the couch and watched *American Pie*. We gasped, groaned, and laughed out loud together. I had to admit, it was funnier than I remembered, and there were plenty of teachable moments—opportunities for me to make sure she knew what all the sexual expressions and slang meant. A few of the best lessons came in the form of karma, when a couple of the guys who tried to exploit and use women for their own ego gratification and status elevation met with some humiliating consequences. All in all, I felt like it worked, and most importantly, we were able to talk about sex, giggle together, and have fun with it.

A few days later, we were talking and laughing about the movie again and I said, "Even though I admit that the movie has some funny and realistic scenarios, there's so much more than this that I want you to know."

Then I continued, "I want to tell you another story, one about the way it used to be. I want to tell you about the goddess Aphrodite."

Aphrodite, Goddess of Love and Beauty

Long ago, in ancient Greece, a golden-haired, green-eyed goddess emerged from the sea and graced the shore of the island of Cyprus. She walked barefoot through the sand, delighting in the sensation of the fine grains between her toes. She smiled as the gentle breezes caressed her cheeks and she raised her face to receive the kiss of the sun. Who was this rare beauty? Where did she come from? With one glance, the fishermen who pulled their nets onto the pebbled beach knew she was a goddess. Radiant in the sunlight, she appeared to be filled with gold. It was whispered among them that she had come from an exotic, faraway place, though others told the tale that she was conceived by the sky and the ocean and rose from the sea on a shell. They called her Aphrodite and worshipped her as the goddess of love and beauty.

Aphrodite delighted in her life among the mortals. She had come to teach them of the many pleasures of love, and she possessed a magical ability to inspire attractions and couplings

With your daughter, visit your local bath and body shop and help her select some sensually delightful products to honor and nurture her Aphrodite Graces—Flowering, Growth, Beauty, Joy, and Radiance. Bath oils, body lotions, and aromatherapy body mists scented with jasmine, lavender, and rose essences are divine!

among all living creatures. In her presence, men and women saw each other in a new light, and even the birds flew off in pairs, gaily chirping new songs. The women often returned with new life within their wombs, blessed by Aphrodite's magic touch.

On the eve of the full moon, Aphrodite could often be found bathing in the sacred waters of Paphos, where, according to stories, she was attended by maidens she lovingly called her Graces. Their names were Flowering, Growth, Beauty, Joy, and Radiance, and they were surrounded by doves. Bathing in the moonlight renewed her spirit for the joyful work she had come to do.

At her sacred temple, beautiful young priestesses, who had learned from Aphrodite that a man need never possess a woman, served the goddess. These priestesses had strong, independent, feminine spirits and each remained "virgin," meaning "one to herself," respected by others and true to their own desires. They honored and lovingly cared for their bodies, they delighted in sensual pleasures, and they knew that pure sexuality was an act of divine love that was to be held sacred.

◐○◑

This is the kind of goddess—one who is true to herself—that I would like to encourage and teach my daughter to be. Aphrodite, the goddess of love and beauty, might be one of the best role models for our daughters as they come of age and discover their sexuality.

KNOWLEDGE IS POWER

Even today, in a culture that is saturated with sex and sexual innuendo, many mothers are reluctant to give their daughters information about sex. But like it or not, our children are being educated and informed. It is our responsibility to provide a safe and loving atmosphere in which to explore the often confusing onslaught of information they receive from educators, friends, and the media.

Knowledge is power. Informed and therefore empowered girls make informed and powerful choices. Contrary to some misconceptions, sexual knowledge does not lead to sexual activity. The hormones that infuse a coming-of-age girl's body arouse her sexually and awaken her sexual desire, and she needs and deserves to understand these new sensations and healthy changes that are happening within her body.

Ruth Bell and her coauthors wrote their book *Changing Bodies, Changing Lives* because they "believe that teenagers —and all of us—have a right to accurate and thorough information about sex." In a note to parents, they state: "Many parents have an underlying feeling that sex information will shock or disturb their children, or even worse that it will interest them TOO much. Some fear that by giving teenagers information about sex, we encourage them to rush out and 'do it.' That isn't what happens. Good sex education makes young people think before acting. Sex education about real people going through real-life situations doesn't make anybody want to go out and get wild."

There are many opportunities to discuss sexuality with our daughters and many moments we need to take advantage of on a day-to-day basis.

"How's your health-science class going?" I asked Austin one day. I like to know what she is being taught and how she is assimilating the information. "You know, I'm actually learning a lot," she told me, with confidence in her voice. I could sense the empowerment she was feeling as she gained new knowledge and her earlier confusion fell away.

From time to time Austin will check out a fact or two with me when she needs clarification. We've definitely opened up and expanded our channel of communication on the subject of sex, and have moved beyond the facts to some critical questions and choices.

MOTHER–DAUGHTER ACTIVITY
Collecting Seashells— The Symbol of Aphrodite

According to myth, Aphrodite was born from the sea. She is often depicted standing on a scallop shell and the seashell is now one of her symbols. With your daughter, find a shell at the beach or an import or gift shop. Place it on your altar to symbolize your divine Aphrodite nature and your sacred sexuality, love, and beauty. Let it be a reminder of all that you know to be true about love and sexuality.

VIRGINITY TODAY

For my daughter, one of the most interesting parts of the sex-education class involves the "anonymous-question box." She and her classmates get to write down questions on slips of paper and put them in a box. Then the teacher previews the questions, reads certain ones out loud, and answers them in front of the class. According to Austin, one of the most common questions is when to have sex for the first time. The question of when is a complex one. "At what age can I have sex and not be considered a slut?" girls wonder. "At what point is it uncool to still be a virgin, and should I just get it over and done with?" When, for goddess's sake, is it okay for a girl to experience and enjoy her sexuality with someone else?

Today's culture narrowly defines what is acceptable and expected of young women. Virginity has become a defining sexual status, and for girls it can be a no-win situation. Either side of the threshold can be a place of embarrassment and shame. Many girls today use sexuality and intercourse as a rite of passage, even though they may have little or no preparation. And that first experience becomes a defining moment, one from which they conceive of their sexual self and create their own personal story.

Our daughters have the right to say yes to healthy, respectful, and honoring relationships and to intimate friendships and loving connections. And they always have the right to say no to anything that does not honor and respect their feelings, hearts, bodies, and souls.

When I asked my friend Nancy what she would like her daughters to understand before having their first sexual experience, she adamantly replied, "I want my daughters to understand that who you let touch your body and into your body is receiving an honor. It's an invitation into your inner world and you should make sure that the invitation is yours.

We get to say, 'Now I'm opening up to you. Let's see what we can create together.' I want them to know that the things we can control, we should, especially who and how we love."

Nancy's daughters are lucky to receive such clear and powerful messages about sexuality. These are precisely the kinds of loving and nonjudgmental messages we need to give our daughters. As mothers we have the power to respond to the mixed and confusing messages our daughters receive today.

Society has created a culture in which we are in a way sexual voyeurs, simply because we don't take the time to relate sex to ourselves. We have compartmentalized what we see from what we do, even though those images from television and radio still stick with us. The other day I picked up my teenage daughter and her girlfriends after a teen seminar on sexuality and relationships. Unlike Austin's class, this group focused more on the whys and why-nots, rather than on the how-to's. Although the girls liked the class and were learning quite a bit about themselves and their sexuality, they described the class as "so sexual—everything is about sex." At the same time, they were singing along in the car to a popular song playing on the radio that explicitly described the male singer cheating on his girlfriend, right down to the details on the many places in which they had sex. When I pointed out the discrepancy between too much sex in class versus the amount of sexual messages on the radio, they were surprised, saying, "Oh, that's different, it's not about us." Technically they were right, but they have become so accustomed to it that they no longer pay attention to any subliminal messages in popular songs.

During the moon groups, we spent one session talking about virginity, sex, and the pressures of growing up in today's sexualized culture. The girls in my groups

Just for Mothers

In your journal or with a good friend, consider some of the following questions:

"What do you recall about your first sexual experience?" "What were some of the earliest messages you received from your parents, friends, teachers, and church or religion about sex?" "What was your overall feeling about sex when you were growing up?" "How do you feel about your sexuality today?" "What would you like your daughter to know about her sexuality?"

laughed in disbelief when I told them that during the '50s and '60s, TV husbands and wives slept in separate beds and rarely kissed on the lips. Nowadays, animated Disney movies reveal even more than that. And in many ways, this openness is better. Husbands and wives do sleep together and kiss on the lips. But we need to combine the seeing with talking. The openness should not be only in the visual images, but in our discussions as well. The discussions in my moon groups were quite different, depending on the ages of the girls. For example, in the groups that consisted of ten- and eleven-year-olds, the discussions were less personal. Most of the girls looked at sex as a concept rather than something that they would ever experience. But in the group of thirteen-year-olds, the discussion was a little more "real." Though none of the girls were sexually active yet, their hormones had begun to kick in and they were more aware of having sexual feelings. (And of course, this varied from girl to girl and group to group.)

The older girls were better able to identify their feelings and with some discussion, better able to articulate them.

"I don't know what it will be like or how I will feel. I don't know when or how it will happen," shared Marina, a thirteen-year-old member of the moon group. "What I do know now is that I want to be ready. And the most important thing is that I want it to be special. I'm worth it."

RECLAIMING OUR SACREDNESS

Talking to our daughters and preparing them for their sexual relationships is not just about giving them information. It may be necessary to first examine our own beliefs about sexuality.

If we are not comfortable being open, honest, and direct in answering our daughters' questions about sexuality, this might provide an opportunity for us to seek out our own sexual healing.

Taking an honest and compassionate look at our own sexual histories, beliefs, and experiences can be the true beginning of our own daughters' healthy sexual development. Admittedly, this is not necessarily easy, and for some of us, especially if we have experienced sexual traumas or abuses in the past, it may be quite difficult and might require the gentle assistance of a therapist or a wise mentor.

"Perhaps the most important source of feelings toward sexuality and about a girl's own body comes from messages from her mother," believes Lonnie Barbach, author and internationally recognized expert on female sexuality. "If a mother approaches life positively and freely and then shares her enthusiasm and love, if she holds aspirations for her daughters which move beyond the confines of traditional roles, then it is likely that the child will develop in a less inhibited, more optimistic, self-sufficient, and independent way."

It's never too late to reclaim our own sexuality, embody the Aphrodite within us, and become a wise teacher and role model for our daughters.

MOTHER–DAUGHTER INTIMACY

Though this chapter is primarily about romantic and sexual love, there are many other kinds of love. One of the most intimate of these is mother love. Mother love is the foundation of our daughters' relationships with others.

When was the last time you held your daughter on your lap, stroked her hair, and caressed her cheek? How often do you put your arms around her while sitting next to each other on the couch, or lay next to her and cuddle in bed? Though at this age, they may be outgrowing their jeans and shoes on a monthly basis, they never outgrow the need to be

MOTHER–DAUGHTER ACTIVITY
Love Letters

In whatever way feels most comfortable, write or tell your daughter all of the ways she is lovable. Notice her qualities rather than her actions. For example, tell her you love her sense of humor or her kindheartedness. She'll likely return the note, without any prompting.

lovingly held and gently touched. This is intimacy. Look her in the eyes when you talk. Listen with your heart. Comfort and reassure her. Treat her with kindness and respect. Be gentle. Respect her boundaries and her right to privacy. Honor her truths and wishes.

Like a pebble dropped in a pond, the mother–daughter connection ripples beyond its center, extending outward to those it touches. It is a gift and a legacy for our whole lives.

The Modern-Day Aphrodite

The modern-day Aphrodite is a virgin goddess, meaning that she is true to her deepest self. She makes conscious choices that honor her body, heart, and soul. She knows that true intimacy is an open, honest, and close relationship with someone she can trust. She values intimate friendships and relationships and understands the difference between intimacy and sexuality. She is empowered with knowledge about her body and about sex. She knows that her sexuality is sacred.

10

Moon Circle

Weaving the Web
of Community

●○◐◑●

Janet and I have known each other for almost two decades. We first met seventeen years ago when we worked together administrating our countywide Head Start program. We lived across the street from each other for ten years. When Janet's babies were born, I acted as a second mother to both of her daughters. I helped her find the most comfortable nursing position and showed her how to give Austin her first bath. Janet helped me connect to my true self and led the way as I searched for deeper meaning in my life. We cared for each other and for each other's children for many years, and we created quite a remarkable community with several other young mothers and families who lived on our street.

Our appreciation for this remarkable community grew throughout the years. We survived divorce, illness, and the death of one of the children in our community. We supported each other. We offered lifelines to each other. We shared parenting tips and child-care responsibilities. We laughed and cried together. We got together for birthdays and holidays and we held annual block parties. We were a community built on shared experiences, understanding,

"Human kind has not woven the web of life. We are but one thread within it. Whatever we do to the web, we do to our selves. All things are bound together. All things connect."

Chief Seattle

and love, and we celebrated our community's spirit in every way we could imagine.

One summer, "picnic night" was born, out of a shared desire to literally step outside of our own little boxes and enjoy the beauty of our greater community together. With several other mothers, we would make some easy, portable dinners, pack up our kids, and head for one of the nearby beaches or parks. Though we are all food enthusiasts, the focus and thread of our informal gatherings was the supportive, communal feeling we were creating in our own true-to-nature, female way.

"Come as you are and bring whatever," was our collective mantra, and that's what we did. Keeping it simple kept it going, and we counted and relied on that. Sometimes we were joined by our male partners and spouses, though the gatherings attracted primarily women and children, and the spirit was truly feminine. One evening during the first summer of picnic night, as we were heading out for Shoreline Park, Patti's husband, Bill, in his perceptive and humorous way, appealed for an invitation with the promise, "I'll bring my feminine side."

Eventually we outgrew our little houses and moved to different parts of the city. We still get together for our dinner reunions, though, and the feeling of community is still there. Though we live in different neighborhoods, the community we created remains in our hearts.

THE WEB OF LIFE

"Far into the night, while the other creatures slept, Charlotte worked on her web. First she ripped out a few of the orb lines near the center. She left the radial lines alone, as they were needed for support. As she worked, her eight legs were a great help to her. So were her teeth. She loved to weave and she was an expert at it."
—E. B. White, *Charlotte's Web*

When we weave our lives together with other women, children, and families, we expand our source of support and create stronger safety nets for our daughters. Women have an innate understanding of the web of interconnectedness and the need for cooperation and community spirit for survival. And no living creature on earth understands the nature of the web better than the spider.

Spider Woman, also known as Grandmother Spider, is the Navajo Indian's goddess of weaving. According to her legends, Spider Woman taught the Navajo women how to weave on a loom, an art that has been passed down from generation to generation. The colorful rugs they still weave today sustain their lives, enrich their culture, and depict the many strands of their lives.

The Myth of the Spider Woman, Goddess of Weaving

There once was a time long, long ago when the Navajo people did not know how to weave, and so they lived in perpetual winter. And though the seasons changed, they always felt the cold of fear in their bones. They worried about their children and the survival of their community. One day, two brave women decided to leave the camp and go out in search of help. They headed into a canyon and found a quiet place where they stopped to pray. Almost immediately the silence was shattered by the sound of a thunderous voice calling down from the top of the canyon wall.

"I hear your prayers and I will help you," echoed the voice of Spider Woman throughout the canyon.

The women were startled and looked up at the woman who stood over them. They had never seen her before and yet her presence felt familiar. They somehow knew that she was one of them, related by time and place, and they gazed at her as she stood above them.

"Our people are cold and hungry," they told her, "and we need food and warmth for our families."

"Yes, I know," replied Spider Woman. "I've been waiting for you to come to me. It's time for you to learn. I will help you, but first you must weave me a rug." And she spun out a long web and lassoed the two women, pulling them up to where she stood over the canyon.

"First, I will build the loom." She spun out another long strand of netlike webbing and lassoed first one pine tree, then another, and stripped them of their branches. Then she planted their trunks firmly into the ground, creating two parallel poles.

"First you must build up, and then across," she instructed. She placed two more poles across the top and bottom until she had a frame. "With this loom, you will learn to weave."

"We don't have time to weave a rug," they told her. "We must return to our families with food and blankets. Please, won't you give us what we need?"

"You will return with all that you need, and more," she assured them, and began to gather materials. With another strand of her web, she lassoed sheep from the canyon below and sheared off their fleecy coats, then showed the women how to wash and card the wool. Together, they spun the wool into yarn. With another mighty strand of her web, Spider Woman began to gather colors from the earth and sky. She took purple from the mountains, blue from the sky, green from the treetops, black from the dark clouds, red from the hot desert sand, white from the moon and the stars, and yellow from the desert yucca plant. The women dyed the wool with all the colors of their world.

"Now you are ready to weave," Spider Woman informed them. "The most important thing to remember, above all else, is to hold only the most beautiful thoughts in your mind as you weave. You must weave from your heart and your soul." And with these few, simple instructions, the women began to weave, threading the colorful wool from east to west, back and forth through the vertical strings. They passed the weft over and under the warps in a rhythmic pattern, holding only the most beautiful thoughts in their heads, and did not notice that Spider Woman had gone.

When the rug was finally complete, the women sat back and admired their work, and Spider Woman returned. "We have woven your rug," the women told her. "And now will you help our families?"

"You have everything you need now to help your families and sustain your lives for generations to come. The gift of weaving has always been and will always be yours. Take it back to your people."

The women returned to their camp and immediately began teaching their people to weave beautiful rugs with all the colors of their world. They were able to trade their rugs for food and warm animal-skin blankets, and soon they had everything they needed and their lives were prosperous. A year later, the two women returned to the canyon to find Spider Woman and thank her for the gift. But they never saw her again.

◑○◐

Spider Woman, the archetypal weaver of the web and creator of life, shows up in other myths and stories, in a variety of forms and disguises. "In mythologies all over the world," notes Sally Helgesen, author of *The Female Advantage—Women's Ways of Leadership*, "female deities are depicted at the loom, knitting together the fabric of human life, spinning out the thread that links the events of the past with the potentialities of the future. The image of weaving is one of the most ancient associated with the female domain."

MOTHER–DAUGHTER ACTIVITY
Weaving

Weave a simple web with your daughter. You will need three slender sticks (bamboo skewers, Popsicle sticks, or small twigs) as well as some yarn or thick string in assorted colors. Cross the three sticks so that they are evenly spaced, then begin to wrap the yarn around them in a circular motion. Change colors and directions as many times as you like. (These are similar to the two-stick "God's eyes" that you may have made at summer camp.)

If you would like to expand your weaving skills, craft stores have tabletop looms, materials, and guidebooks. Your community may also offer weaving classes through adult education programs or at local craft and fiber-arts stores.

With your daughter, name
three women that you each
admire, either historical,
famous, known, or unknown
figures. (For example:
Joan of Arc, Anne Frank,
or a grandmother.) Describe
what you admire about each
woman and why her part-
icular qualities are important
to you.

TEACHING OUR DAUGHTERS TO WEAVE A COMMUNITY

Spider Woman, the goddess of weaving, offered the women in the story a greater gift than they imagined. She told them to "hold only beautiful thoughts in your mind while you weave a rug" and to "weave from your soul." Not until they returned to their families did they discover that by learning how to weave, they had received a greater gift than they had asked for. To ease their people's suffering, they began to teach them to gather wool, color it with dyes, and weave wool into rugs. They had developed new skills and resources to sustain and enrich their lives. Their gift increased in value when they shared it with others.

Like Spider Woman, we can give our daughters the skills to "weave their own rugs" and pass on the knowledge of how to create an interconnected web of life and become part of a supportive community, during the coming-of-age years and beyond.

MOON MENTORS

In many professions, we have teachers, mentors and guides, and it is equally important that we provide them for our daughters. Emma, my thirteen-year-old daughter, has chosen a mentor to guide her through her coming-of-age program. Once a week, they get together over hot chocolate to talk about shared values and the connections in their lives. On Saturday mornings they volunteer together at the local food bank, delivering food to needy families. They are planning a vision quest and a coming-of-age service with the other coming-of-agers and group leaders in Emma's Unitarian Universalist program. Her mentor, Nancy, can provide her with an additional voice of woman's wisdom and is an invaluable source of support and guidance.

Nancy is a physical therapist with three children of her own. Although Nancy and I are good friends and often mother together, sharing carpools and children, Nancy has become even more important and special in Emma's life. The commitment that Nancy has made by becoming Emma's mentor has given their relationship a new depth and meaning. And I have had the pleasure of mentoring Nancy's oldest daughter, Christyn. Although it has been four years since I was Christyn's mentor, our bond goes beyond the friendship of our families, and there is a special place in my heart for Christyn. She knows that I am only a phone call or e-mail away, and Nancy and Emma share the same bond. Nancy's voice blends with mine and those of the other wise women in Emma's life. Mentorships can begin without any prior knowledge of each other. In Emma's coming-of-age group, there are several newly formed relationships that are thriving. There can never be too many sources of comfort, support, and guidance for our daughters as they tread the waters of adolescence.

There is an African adage that says: "It takes a village to raise a child." Creating community is a conscious act and a feminine value that reflects our tribal roots and communal nature. By surrounding our daughters with the voices of women, we are consciously re-creating villages for our daughters.

GIRLFRIENDS

As we all know, friendships between women are crucial to the feminine well-being. The friendships of preadolescent and adolescent girls are particularly important. At a time when girls might feel that their mothers can't possibly understand what they are going through, they can still relate to their friends. They provide each other with the comfort of shared feelings and experiences. Recently, Austin

---

MOTHER–DAUGHTER ACTIVITY
Mentors and Role Models

Who are the wise women and powerful female role models in your daughter's life? Choosing a mentor, teacher, or other wise woman can provide an additional and essential source of support for your daughter. Who else can she talk to? Who does she trust? With your daughter, identify the other wise women in her life. Encourage her to connect with another woman who could act as a mentor. Mentor activities can include community service, movie dates, and talking over hot chocolate.

With your daughter, talk about the most valuable friendships you have each had in your life. Acknowledge the value of your different friendships. Choose a special friend that each of you would like to acknowledge, then write a letter to that person. Let your friends know how much their friendship means to you. Acknowledge the many ways they support and understand you. Share with them some of your favorite memories of your friendship.

told me that seventh grade is about finding your place and your group.

Girlfriends, at every age, are essential points of connection in our ever-changing and often challenging lives.

FRIENDS FOR LIFE

On a glass-top table on my in-laws' patio in Arizona sits a blue terra-cotta statue. Four clay figures stand together in a circle with their arms around each other, surrounding a candle. When I asked about it during our last Christmas visit, my mother-in-law, Millie, told me that it was given to her by her friend Pat. The statue has a tag attached to it with a story entitled, "The Circle of Friends Myth."

It says: "Since the beginning of time, friendship has been the most important relation that woman has experienced. According to the myth, ancient women used to gather around a new fire to celebrate peace and sisterhood among the tribes. The legend tells that if you give a circle of friends to a person you care for, your bonds of friendship will endure forever."

When I asked my mother-in-law if Pat had given it to her for a special occasion, she said, "No, no particular occasion, just because that's what we do. If we see something that we think the other might like, we just buy it and give it to each other." The circle-of-friends statue represents many special, long-term friendships in Millie's life. "One of my best buds is Judy," she told me, "who I've known since I was twenty-nine years old." She paused a moment. "We've been friends for forty-four years." Though they live across the country from each other, they talk on the phone and e-mail each other all the time. Millie and her friend Jan have also known each other for more than forty years. They taught in the same school district, golfed and cross-country skied together, and sailed together on Lake Michigan. They still see each other as often as they can and they talk on the phone every day. Her other friend, Ruth, is a friend of forty-three years and loves Millie's children like her own. Several of Millie's friends were like second mothers to her children, Robin, Kim, and Ted. "We share a lot of secrets, wishes, and desires," she told me about her closest friends, "as women so often do." Millie has a strong circle of friends, old and new, and in the pictures that are all over her refrigerator, these women are posed much like the statue on her patio table, with their arms draped around each other's shoulders. "I love my lady friends—all of them," she told me with a warm smile.

REGROUPING—THE CIRCLE IS CAST AGAIN

Our angel group gathers together about four times a year to list our hopes on index cards and share them with each other. We listen to each other and promise to hold those wishes and dreams for each other. Elizabeth meets every month with her book group. Although they do actually read and discuss books, they spend time each month talking about relationships, family, and their worries and triumphs. Lucinda hosts a full-moon circle each month for women to remember their connection to the moon and its cycles.

As we reawaken to our goddess heritage, we are recasting our own circles and reweaving our webs of community. For centuries, women have been meeting together in groups, forming quilting bees and sewing circles, and recently we have been making spirituality the focus of our gatherings. Coming together to explore our female values and connect with our feminine soul has once again become an essential source of inspiration, guidance, and support as we collectively redefine our female selves and reshape and transform our lives.

At a time when so many of us are awakening to a new feminine consciousness and to intuitive knowing, women's groups and circles have become the container for our shared discoveries and explorations as we seek new ways to live our own lives and to guide and empower our daughters.

The girls who participated in my summer moon groups had their first experiences of celebrating their spirituality together. In a sacred space and intimate setting, they were more easily able to open up to each other and talk about the things that matter and about what they truly think about in their own quiet, reflective time. They talked about their bodies, their feelings, their fears, and their triumphs. Through journal writing and discussions, they explored their intuition and shared their dreams. The girls loved that group connection. It nourished their souls and empowered their journeys. And it reminded them that they are goddesses.

MOTHER–DAUGHTER CIRCLES

Though most of the original families and mothers have since left our first neighborhood, we still get together as often as possible for a women's night out. We laugh ourselves silly reminiscing about our earlier challenges, but we also seriously acknowledge that we don't know how we would have done it without each other. All of our children had the benefit of extra mothers, and still do, which feels just as important during the coming-of-age years. Now that our daughters are older, picnic night has evolved and is now a monthly mother–daughter dinner club. These are gatherings filled with food, laughter, love, and storytelling. And anytime we consider skipping a dinner meeting, our daughters always insist that we honor our tradition.

The Modern-Day Spider Woman

Today's Spider Woman, the goddess of weaving, is a creator of community. She understands the interconnectedness of all living things. She knows the value of interdependence and creates mutually beneficial relationships in order to both give and receive support. She sees community as a safety net and an expanded source of support for herself, her daughter, and her loved ones. She knows that asking for help is a sign of strength and confidence, and that helping others nourishes her soul and helps to complete the circle. She lives with a spirit of cooperation.

11
Moon Gift
Giving Back to the World

●◐○◐●

What are your authentic gifts? What are you called to do? What can you give because of your authentic gifts? My friend Melitta pondered these questions for years, struggling through adversity to discover her unique gifts and to find her purpose. It wasn't until the final days of her life that she was able to see clearly that she was an inspiration. At the eulogy her husband gave at her funeral, he told her friends and loved ones, "During the last few weeks of her life, Melitta began to realize that she was truly unique, with a purpose and a special gift. She saw how her cancer experience healed the personal relationships of herself and others. She saw how her struggles triggered strong emotions of love and compassion that she hadn't seen before from her friends and family. She saw her difficulties bring men to hug each other who never had before! She saw friends and family join together and share feelings that were, before, too uncomfortable to talk about. She saw friends and family look inside themselves and ponder their own lives and priorities. She saw all these things and she knew that it was her struggles and her courage that was changing people's lives. She

"No other woman on earth can do what you alone are called to do, can give to the world what you alone were sent to give through your authentic gifts. The call may be so faint you can barely make out the message, but if you listen, you will hear it."

Sarah Ban Breathnach,
Simple Abundance—A Daybook of Comfort and Joy

realized that she was the catalyst and inspiration for these changes. This gave her what she was always looking for, her entire life: A PURPOSE!"

Unfortunately, especially for those of us who miss Melitta's physical presence, it was in death that she discovered her purpose. Her spirit and the purpose of that spirit remain with those of us who were blessed to have known her. She guides us in our work and service to others.

In mythology, the heroine's journey begins with a call. It is usually a call to adventure, to explore something not yet known, or to challenge oneself to discover hidden strengths and abilities. The call often asks us to step outside ourselves and our comfort zones, to reach deeper within ourselves, and to give something of ourselves. In our own lives, the call can be heard as a loud wake-up call, perhaps one initiated by a crisis such as an illness, accident, or loss, urging us to become more aligned with our purpose. But it can also be a faint whisper, quietly beckoning us to become more active and visible with our gifts.

Each of us has our own unique gifts and calling, something special to contribute to the world. Our call may come in several forms and our journeys may change over the course of our lives. Our life purpose might be the work we were trained to do, or it might be that we must quit a successful career so we can do what we love, much like Lynn with her mosaic business. For a significant time in our lives, we may choose to stay home with our children. When my friend Jody, for example, had almost completed her master's in educational psychology, she became pregnant with her second child and decided to take a break from her training to become a marriage and family counselor. That was fourteen years ago. On her tax return, she now lists her occupation as "house goddess" and that is precisely what she is! She has consciously chosen to put her career on hold in order to homeschool her children, because that has become her calling. As her daughters approach adulthood, she has begun looking into ways in which she can restart her career. My friend Carolyn, the mother of two young children, has just completed her first year of seminary school. Carolyn is now juggling her family life and her studies in order to fulfill her purpose. The weekly commute, the homework, and the time away from her family are sacrifices she is willing to make. Ministry is a calling she could not ignore.

Melitta's death eight years ago inspired me to look inside myself and to discover my own truths, gifts, and purpose. After her death, the same questions that had inspired her journey became my own, and I, too, wanted to know my purpose.

Guided by intuition and a series of undeniable signs and coincidences, I converted my garage into a small and beautiful studio, with enough space for groups of women to sit comfortably and with a desk and a computer I had won in a friend's office lottery. In a private practice I call Soul Work, my call from then on has been to help other women discover their true selves, gifts, and purposes, a process I have been refining both personally and professionally for years. My work with women, coupled with a desire to share these discoveries with my daughters, led to the formation of the moon groups for girls—a little soul work for mothers and daughters together.

SOUL WORK—DISCOVER YOUR GIFTS AND PURPOSE

Every New Year's Eve, the adults in our homeschooling community gather to have dinner. It is a potluck of gourmet dishes, without the obligatory macaroni and cheese that our children require at our usual gatherings. It has become a wonderful way to connect, think about the year ahead, and

In your journals or out loud, name five imaginary lives you would like to lead. Remember that you are using your imagination and anything is possible. If you would like to, write or describe "a day in the imaginary life," using the first-person present tense. Begin with "I am a..." and see where it takes you. Notice how you feel as you do this exercise.

plan what we hope to accomplish. In our quest to make it until midnight and celebrate the new year, we have turned our after-dinner conversation into a game of imagination. One year, we talked about which famous person, living or dead, we would most like to meet and why. The conversation was lively and fun. This year we took a more serious look at our own lives by talking about an imaginary life we might like to have. Imagining what we might have led us to think outside our normal lives and showed us new ways to share our gifts and talents.

When I offer this exercise to the women and girls in my groups, I ask them to write about one of their imaginary lives in the first-person present tense. For example: "I am a documentary filmmaker and I create films about nature and the environment." One opening line can lead to pages of insight and an outpouring of new ideas.

Female Gifts

In her book *The Shadow King—The Invisible Force that Holds Women Back*, Sidra Stone describes a dream she had that gave her awareness of her female gifts:

"In my dream I am carrying a large parcel of important women's 'treasures.' This must be delivered to a group where men and women work together as partners in a new kind of partnership. There is no path. As I walk, my footing often gives way and the rocks slide out from beneath my feet. I must concentrate all my consciousness upon the moment, upon the placement of my feet at each step. I must relate to my body and to the earth. If not, I will not be able to complete my task. Only men have passed this way before, and they conquered by will, pushing beyond barriers, by brute force. They succeeded in reaching their goals, but they carried nothing of the feminine with them. I must reach the goal in a new way and, as I struggle towards it, I must not drop any of my female gifts."

Beneath our imaginary lives often lie the gifts that are uniquely ours and are not as easily accessed. As we discussed in Chapter 5, sometimes our divine gifts and purposes are revealed to us in our dreams.

So far in this chapter, our focus has been on discovering our daughters' and our own purpose—to connect to our life's work. But we can also find purpose and meaning in compassionate service, much like the goddess Kwan Yin did.

The Myth of Kwan Yin—Divine Mother of Compassion

Long ago in ancient China, there lived a beautiful young maiden with skin as white and translucent as a pearl, hair as black and radiant as onyx, and eyes that sparkled like two tigereye stones. Her mother died when she was just a babe in arms, so, along with her two older sisters, she was raised by a cruel and demanding father. He had little interest in his three daughters, except to marry them off to wealthy husbands who would offer him greater status and social advantage.

Kwan Yin's early life was not easy, and she suffered in pain and hardship. As her sisters came of age, her father found for them two of the wealthiest young men in the land, and with no concern for the young men's temperaments, the father arranged for his daughters' marriages. Kwan Yin loved her sisters deeply, as they had cared for her like mothers since she was a baby. When she saw how unkindly her sisters were treated by their husbands, even on the day that they were wed, she felt great pain and compassion for them and wanted desperately to avoid a similar fate. She knew that the only respectable alternative to marriage was to enter a temple and offer her life in service.

As she approached the suitable age for marriage, Kwan Yin found the courage to ask her father to allow her to enter a nearby temple and live out her life in service. When he saw the determination in his daughter's dark eyes, he reluctantly agreed, but he gave orders to the temple residents to put his daughter through the harshest tests in order to shake her conviction. She was forced to work day and night. But in her earlier years, Kwan Yin had befriended the animals that lived near her home and around the temple, so when they saw the relentless daily drudgery she had been forced to endure, they came to her assistance.

With the help of her animal friends, Kwan Yin was able to accomplish her tasks with remarkable ease and a newfound joy, and her feats appeared miraculous. The news of Kwan Yin's accomplishments reached her father and he became enraged. He crept into the temple one night and set fire to the room in which Kwan Yin slept. She woke from her light sleep and quickly put out the fire with her bare hands; miraculously, she did not have any burns. This infuriated her father even more and he ordered her to be put to death for disobedience.

Kwan Yin died without fear and peacefully entered a state of heaven. The purity and unconditional love within her own heart transformed her into a goddess, and Kwan Yin vowed to return to earth and continue her life of service, forever working to ease the pain and suffering of her beloved humanity.

Kwan Yin is revered in China as the divine mother of compassion. She embodies the principle of *karuna*, boundless compassion and the spirit of loving kindness. She sits upon a lotus flower, the symbol of enlightenment, with a baby in her arms. Calling Kwan Yin's name is believed to bring protection and compassion.

◐○◑

The goddess Kwan Yin inspires compassionate service. As women, much of our lives are about caring for others— our children, our partners, and later, our aging parents. Compassion and empathy are feminine values that can be encouraged and developed through community service and volunteering.

COMMUNITY SERVICE AND VOLUNTEERING—
MAKING A CONTRIBUTION

There are many ways to make a difference. Sometimes we give our time, energy, or service, sometimes we donate money, and sometimes we literally give blood.

After September 11, I decided that one of the contributions I could and would like to make to my community was to give blood. I have the universal blood type O with the more rare Rh-negative factor. I committed myself to offering my blood every fifty-six days, which is as often as is medically possible. I confess, I missed my donation last month and told myself that because I was writing this book, I didn't have the time. But yesterday, the phone rang. It was the blood bank, urgently seeking my blood type and asking me if I could come in for an hour. "An hour?" I thought to myself, looking out the window at my neglected dog, yard, and life. And then I remembered why I had committed myself as a blood donor. This is community service. And an hour of time and a pint of blood every fifty-six days are definitely things I can spare.

There are many ways to make a difference. Mothers and daughters walk together in honor of loved ones or to raise money for breast-cancer research. Families make dinners for the local homeless shelter, helping to prepare and deliver the meals. A group of women gather around the table at a board meeting each month to actively support their favorite cause.

THE CALL TO COMMUNITY SERVICE

Community service, volunteering, and making a contribution are themes that emerge and take on more meaning as girls come of age. The call to service—to give of oneself and give back to the world—is heard from within as well as from the greater outside community.

In today's public education system, a new program called Service Learning is being introduced to young people. The intention of the program is to make learning more meaningful and to connect young people to their community. The key concept here is that of meaningful service. The service being offered must be meaningful to the provider as well as to the community, which creates a meaningful relationship and connection between a young person and her community. Two other important elements of the program are reflection and celebration. Participants are encouraged to reflect, both publicly and privately, on their service project, using forms of expression such as writing, speaking, drawing, singing, and photography. The students are then recognized and celebrated for their contribution by people who are important in their lives as well as in the greater community.

Many schools today also require students to contribute a certain number of community-service hours in order to graduate from high school. Following the model of the Service Learning program is an ideal way to present the concept of meaningful service to a girl and her community.

Performing meaningful community service creates a strong relationship between a young person and her community, while also fostering a service ethic and kindling a sense of community spirit in her heart.

DO WHAT YOU LOVE

There are many opportunities for service in every community, and oftentimes it can be overwhelming to choose just one cause. One of the best ways to start is to make a list of the things that you and your daughter like to do. Do you love animals or babies? Do you feel an affinity to nature and the environment? Do you like to do things in groups or do you prefer tasks that are individual or with just one or two others?

COMPASSIONATE LISTENING

*"Your work is to discover your work, and then
with all your heart to give yourself to it."*
—Buddha

Thich Nhat Hanh, a Vietnamese monk and teacher known for his compassionate presence and clarity, talks about Kwan Yin in *The Heart of the Buddha's Teaching*. "In Buddhism, Kwan Yin is a person who has a great capacity for listening and true presence. 'Kwan Yin' means 'the one who can listen and understand the sound of the world, the crisis of the suffering.'" The essence of Kwan Yin is compassion and understanding, which are the gifts of those who personify her archetype and embody her spirit. Kwan Yin reminds us to be compassionate listeners to our coming-of-age daughters and inspires compassionate service in all of us.

The Modern-Day Kwan Yin

The modern-day Kwan Yin seeks meaning and purpose in her life. She has a compassionate heart and a community spirit. She finds ways to offer meaningful service to her community. She knows that she has unique gifts to discover and share with others. She celebrates her gifts and gives of herself to the world.

12
Moon Dance
Celebrating Coming-of-Age

●◐○◑●

The week before my daughter Sarah was born, a small group of my closest women friends came to my house one night with gifts, food, and flowers. We gathered in my bedroom, the intended place of her birth. The room was lit with candles and the moonlight from the garden. A soft blanket was spread out on the floor, and in loose, comfortable clothing, I lay down on my back. The women sat in a circle around me, one at my head, one at my feet, and one on each side. From bowls of herb and flower water, they bathed my hands, feet, face, and belly. They sang and read poetry, blessed the space we sat in, and offered good wishes for my baby, our birth, and me. Later, in the dining room, we feasted on pasta, salad, bread, wine, and my favorite chocolate cake.

On the night before my friend's mastectomy, a small group of her women friends gathered together in her living room. We went to support her and witness her as she lovingly acknowledged the value of the breast that she was losing, courageously named everything she was releasing, and tossed inscribed notes into the fire.

"Love, empathy, compassion, and a sense of connectedness, oneness, and unity ... these are precisely the feelings that effective women's rituals create."

Joan Borysenko, *A Woman's Journey to God*

Every night, Tara, a single mother grieving the long illness and then death of her husband, gathers her three children around her before they go to bed, and together they vocalize gratitude for that which gives fullness to their lives.

One Sunday a month, a group of neighborhood women leave their spouses and their children to join together for a dinner filled with wine, laughter, and shared memories.

Ask a room full of women if anyone has ever attended or organized a ritual, and very few hands will go up. Ask these same women if they have ever attended or given a baby shower, birthday party, graduation party, bridal shower, or going-away party, and every hand will go up knowingly and enthusiastically. Rituals are what women know best—it's just that we've stopped calling them that. We call them traditions, celebrations, and parties, and we give them for every occasion imaginable.

Ritual is defined as "the form for a ceremony" or "a customary act." Whether it's an act of worship, a daily walk on the beach, or choosing the same spot in an exercise class every day, we have many rituals in our lives. In our busy days, quite often our rituals are reduced to daily mundane activities and routines—in the absence of meaningful ritual, we now choose to ritualize our routines. While ritual was once an integral part of community, family, and spiritual life and as essential as a nourishing meal, conscious rituals have slipped away, replaced instead by fast-paced acts of busyness, drive-through relationships, empty connections, and other forms of convenience "food."

Conscious ritual is a way to connect, to worship, to heal, and to celebrate. Ritual brings people together and honors the sacred, marking and creating special moments in time. Spiritually, our souls, bodies, and minds crave ritual that has meaning. Rituals can lend a sense of safety, can act as containers for meaningful experiences, and can at the same time create an opportunity for growth and change. Rituals sanctify all aspects of our lives, adding meaning, depth, and time for reflection.

Since antiquity, life has revolved around rituals, and rituals have provided sustenance for life.

The Myth of the Women's Society

The following story contains excerpts from "The Women's Society" and "Stones," reprinted with permission from Daughters of Copper Woman *(Harbour Publishing 2002), a collection of stories passed down by the native people of Vancouver Island and retold by Anne Cameron.*

◑◯◐

People were living almost as they were intended to live. Almost. And the Society of Women was strong. It was intertribal. Open to all women, regardless of age, social status, or wealth.

No woman could buy her way into the society. No woman could inherit a position in the society. Each member of the society had been chosen by the society itself, and invited to join and become one of the sisters. Even the slave women could belong to the society if they were invited, and their owner could not deny them the right to join, nor keep them from the meetings, nor forbid them permission to join in the ceremonies, for the society was powerful, and respected by all.

The education of all girl children was the duty of the members of the Women's Society. They taught with jokes and with songs, with legends and examples, they taught the girls how to care for and enjoy their bodies, how to respect their bodily functions, they explained to them all they would ever need to know about pregnancy, childbirth, and child care.

"When you'd learned everythin' you had to learn, and the time was right, and you'd had your first bleedin' time and been to the waitin' house, there was a big party. You were a woman. And the people would come from other places, uncles and aunts and cousins and friends, and there'd be singin' and dancin' and lots of food. Then they'd take you in a special dugout, all decorated up with water-bird down, the finest feathers off the breast of the bird, and you'd have all your best clothes and all of your crests, and you'd stand up there so proud and happy. And they'd chant a special chant and the old women would lead them, and they'd take you a certain distance. When the chant ended the old woman would sing a special prayer, and take off all your clothes and you'd dive into the water, and the dugout would go home. And you'd be out there in the water all by yourself, and you had to swim back to the village.

The people would watch for you, and they'd light fires on the beach and when they finally saw you they'd start to sing a victory song about how a girl went for a swim and a woman came home. And you'd make it to the beach and your legs would feel like they were made of rocks or somethin'. You'd try to stand up and you would shake all over, just plain wore out. And then the old woman, she'd come up and put her cape over you and you'd feel just fine. And after that you were a woman, and if you wanted to marry up with someone you could, and if you wanted to have children, you could, because you'd be able to take care of them in the proper way."

◖○◗

RITUAL, CELEBRATION, THE WOMEN'S SOCIETY

How would the coming-of-age years be different if every community had a local chapter of the Women's Society? What if our daughters were guided by a wise and respected group of women, rather than by the media or their peers? What if each community had a time-honored way to celebrate each girl as she came of age?

According to Kathleen Wall, co-author of *Rites of Passage—Celebrating Life's Changes*, "Ritual works in three basic ways: It empowers us through action; it clarifies problems, transitions, and new directions; and it helps new perspectives and behaviors take root in our daily lives."

Coming-of-age is a life passage that has been historically celebrated with ritual and linked with menarche, a girl's first period. In indigenous cultures, menstruation meant that new lives would be created and that the tribe would continue and the culture would survive. A coming-of-age ritual was a celebration and an affirmation of life, a way of acknowledging a girl's passage to womanhood and her new ability to bear children.

It's hard to imagine very many girls today, at least in our Western culture, who would want to have a party to celebrate their first periods. There was a time when my daughter would certainly have thought I was nuts to even suggest such a thing. In our current state of world overpopulation, a young girl's ability to bear children is no longer the focus of all coming-of-age rituals. But the physical changes occurring throughout puberty, which overtly mark the coming-of-age years, coincide with deeper, more spiritual changes.

The physiological changes that occur at this time increase and enhance a girl's sense of self. It has been hypothesized that increasing levels of hormones bring greater levels of self-awareness, empathy, and intuition. A coming-of-age girl is more able to experience herself in relation to her greater environment—her community, culture, and the world. Coming-of-age is a time to acknowledge not only her physical changes, but also her spiritual passage and transformation from girlhood to womanhood.

Today, coming-of-age ceremonies are still performed worldwide, in all kinds of cultures. Many people of different religions and spiritual practices are also creating new ceremonies. Though the format may be different from ceremony to ceremony, the intention is similar: to honor and celebrate a young girl at this sacred turning point in her life, to acknowledge her changing role and increasing responsibilities, and to offer her a lifetime of love and support within her community.

A VISION QUEST

The vision quest is an ancient tradition practiced by Native Americans and other indigenous people. It is one of the oldest spiritual journeys, and is used as a rite of passage for both boys and girls. While it usually requires one to leave one's home and go out into the world, the most important part of the journey is inward. After being ritually cleansed by fasting and then tested by nature, the participant is rewarded with a vision of her future that reveals her life's calling or purpose.

When my daughter was preparing for her coming-of-age ceremony, she and a group of other coming-of-agers and leaders embarked on a vision quest. The original plan was to go camping and hiking in our local mountains, but that idea was rained out and the vision quest was relocated to a beach house. Although at first glance it did not seem like a place that would facilitate the intention of a traditional quest, it did just that on many levels. The house was small and the group needed to learn to share space and work and live together. There was the challenge of finding a place to go inward in a physical environment not made for twenty people—modern-day obstacles that we often face. Also, one of the planned exercises was the cooperative construction of a labyrinth. This had to be accomplished in the wind and rain on shifting sand. The group and their mentors then walked the labyrinth, umbrellas and parkas flapping uselessly against the elements. Remarkably, all of the tasks of the vision quest were accomplished, and many of the group came away transformed. This vision quest challenged the group in a way that was more applicable to their modern lives than a solitary stay in a cave in the wilderness could have.

WHAT IS A COMING-OF-AGE CELEBRATION?

As in the Women's Society, traditional adolescent rites of passage share a similar design: preparation with teaching, a test or an initiation (such as a vision quest), and a final celebration with a ceremony and party. What kind of ritual based on ancient practices might you create for a modern girl who is coming of age?

A coming-of-age celebration is usually a ceremony and a party. For some people it is a very serious occasion, a time-honored tradition that features some very specific components. Sometimes it includes a challenge or an initiation of some sort—perhaps a difficult test of personal strength or courage. Some celebrations are small, intimate gatherings with gifts and wishes and promises of support. Some take place in nature, others in churches or formal settings. Some occur as a spontaneous experience and are only acknowledged later upon further reflection.

Coming-of-age celebrations are often held on or around a thirteenth birthday. Many girls will not yet have begun to menstruate by the time they are thirteen, so this is no longer a prerequisite for a coming-of-age celebration. But a thirteenth birthday still marks the beginning of the teenage years, and most girls today are pretty eager to cross this threshold and celebrate their new status. Celebrating at this time provides a great opportunity to emphasize the rights and responsibilities that come with age. The Jewish bat mitzvah is an example of a traditional coming-of-age ceremony that takes place around a girl's thirteenth birthday.

My daughter's friend Marina wrote this description of her bat mitzvah:

My bat mitzvah was a real coming-of-age ceremony for me. It may have been the year of intense preparation, or maybe the actual religious ceremony, but it really seemed to me that I grew up that day. Or took a significant step in that direction anyway. Leading up to my bat mitzvah, it was mostly just a thing to please my grandparents. It was also for me, of course, but I wouldn't have chosen it by myself. As it got closer to the actual date, it got ... well, more real. Especially when I wrote and edited my speech, it started really meaning something to me. At the ceremony, I really seemed to see everything in a slightly different light. I didn't really notice it at the time. I never notice big changes when I'm in the middle of them. Looking back on it, however, I can see that it did change me. Also, that was the first time I got to wear high heels. That made me feel very grown up. It was a very special ceremony, and I'm glad I did it. I feel more Jewish now than I did before.

Coming-of-age, though often marked by a moment or experience, is also a process that occurs over time. Marina's ceremony was the culmination of a year-long process, a journey inward to a deeper knowledge of herself and her heritage. The ceremony itself offered her an opportunity to find meaning in her life, gave her a voice to express it, and let her to wear high heels for the first time.

Some girls come of age not with a specific ceremony but with an event or experience. Jody, a friend of mine in her forties, came of age in the early '70s and did not have an actual ceremony, but she still feels that she had a coming-of-age experience, one that came about through her travels, a vision quest of sorts. This is her story.

In my family, we had no special ceremonies for coming-of-age. I remember the day I started my period as being somewhat anticlimactic. Most of my friends had already begun menstruating and I knew (or thought I knew) all I needed to know. There was nothing dramatic about it—no cramps, no fear, no big rush of blood, no drama. I remember my mom telling my grandmother that I had "become a woman" that day. I didn't feel particularly womanly, actually just embarrassed that my body was being discussed. I was thirteen and I had been wearing a bra for two years for no real reason and had been carrying around a "sanitary napkin and belt" while waiting for my big moment. When it did come, the miracle of it lasted about four hours and then it was like I had been menstruating my whole life. It was very natural for me.

During the summer that I turned fourteen, two friends and I somehow managed to talk our parents into letting us go to Canada for several weeks so that my one friend could visit with her parents, who lived there. The idea of being on our own for the two-day train ride was extremely exciting. I remember waiting at the depot for the train to come. All of our families were there for our big send-off. When the train pulled away, heading north with us on it, I thought we would burst in anticipation. The freedom of that train ride! We walked up and down the cars, we chatted with our fellow travelers, and we ate whatever we wanted from the concession stand.

We managed to transfer successfully from the train to the bus in Seattle for the rest of the trip to Vancouver. My girlfriend's mom lived in the city and worked full-time. So for nearly two weeks, we got around the city on mass transit, which was a new and very big deal for me. We shopped, we went to museums, and we just kicked around, reveling in our freedom. Canada was such a great country to travel in for a first experience alone. They speak English, which made things easy, but we still needed to convert American dollars to Canadian dollars, and sending letters was a bit different than in the states.

From Vancouver we drove to Penticton, which was a much more rural setting. My friend's father lived in a tiny house in an apple orchard and cooked on a wood-burning stove. We pitched a tent out in the orchard and stayed for a week. He worked full-time as well, so again our time was our own. We picked apples and baked apple pies, we packed picnic lunches and hitchhiked to the nearby lake, and we spent the days swimming, diving from rafts, and eating and sleeping to our hearts' content. On the long walk home, we picked cherries from the orchard trees until we could eat no more. During those two weeks, we talked nearly nonstop about boys, our bodies, other people, and especially about what was important.

That was the summer I came of age.

Though she did not have a ceremony, Jody's story shares some similarities with the young girls' rituals in the Women's Society, and even with Marina's bat mitzvah. She and her friends prepared for their journey, they had a big send-off from their families, and they went off on their own to test their ability, maturity, and inner resources. They shared with each other information about boys, their bodies, and other matters of importance. Jody knew her experience had been a transforming one and that she had returned changed, a new and different person.

MODERN CEREMONIES FOR MODERN GIRLS

Nancy, who has two daughters very close in age, had two very different ceremonies for each of them. The first ceremony was for her oldest daughter, Christyn, on her thirteenth birthday. Christyn decided to include a few of her closest friends, several women and men who were important in her life, and her sister, Alisha. She wanted her ceremony to be held at home, so we gathered together and sat in a circle in her living room. The room was decorated with candles and flowers and an altar was in the center. Borrowing from an earth-based spirituality, we first called in the four directions, asking for energy from the north, east, south, and west. Once the circle was cast, we each read passages we had selected for her from different spiritual and religious sources, each one as eclectic as its reader. This was a great example of how a nondenominational ceremony can draw on a variety of traditions and resources, bringing depth and breadth to the ritual. At the end of the ceremony, we presented her with gifts, all of which symbolized her coming-of-age. It was a very moving ceremony and was just how Christyn had wanted it to be. Even the dads in the group needed tissues.

Her sister Alisha's reaction, however, was, "Don't ever do that to me." And her ceremony was as different from Christyn's as the two girls are different from each other. For Alisha, it was most important to be with her friends, so on her thirteenth birthday she had a slumber party and asked all her friends to dress as their favorite movie stars. Unknowingly, they had been preparing for her coming-of-age celebration for several months, as each girl researched the life of a famous woman for a school project. The "guests" that night included Lucille Ball, Vivian Leigh, Audrey Hepburn, Grace Kelly, Katherine Hepburn, and Elizabeth Taylor, and Alisha starred as Marilyn Monroe. In many ways, they were trying on their new roles as women, stepping out of their girlhood and into someone new. As a gift to her sister, Christyn prepared and served a four-course gourmet dinner. Alisha's mother planned a simple midnight ceremony during which each girl presented Alisha with a special bead that they felt best represented her. The beads were later strung into a bracelet. Afterwards, they watched old movies, ate popcorn, and stayed up all night. That was a perfect coming-of-age celebration for her—a blend of family, friends, and fun.

Another mother I know chose to celebrate with her daughter alone and made her queen for a day. They shopped for a new outfit, had facials and manicures, and lunched in a nice restaurant. She read excerpts to her from her baby book and journal. That night, on the girl's thirteenth birthday, her friends came over for a slumber party.

Although all of these ceremonies and coming-of-age parties were very different, the intention was the same—to acknowledge and celebrate each girl as she came of age.

PLANNING FOR YOUR DAUGHTER

How do you create a coming-of-age ritual for your daughter that honors her unique self and also honors your ancestors, family traditions, or faith?

As we learned from Christyn and Alisha, what is right for one girl might be all wrong for another. A coming-of-age ceremony is not intended to further embarrass an already self-conscious adolescent girl! The intention is for it to be both meaningful and enjoyable. To get started, you might find out whether your family or culture has a traditional ceremony or rite of passage. Jewish girls celebrate their coming-of-age with a bat mitzvah and Mexican girls with a quinceañera. Catholics have a confirmation ceremony, and Unitarian Universalists have a coming-of-age program with adult mentors and service projects. Do you belong to a church that has a ceremony you like? Your community may even have someone who organizes coming-of-age ceremonies.

Lucinda Eileen, a woman who specializes in planning coming-of-age ceremonies, helps girls plan their celebrations in a very specific way. She meets with the girl and her family many months before the actual celebration is to take place. For part of the ceremony, she asks the girl, with the help of her family, to learn about the women in her family. For example, what was her great-grandmother's name? How did she live? Was she an immigrant, or maybe part of a family that settled in the West? What kind of hardships did she face? Knowing the history of the women in the family can strengthen a girl's sense of self and provide many insights into the women of the family, such as who they are or were, what they experienced, and why they are the way they are. Much of this information is then used in the ceremony to honor the girl as well as her lineage and origin.

Coming-of-age celebrations come in all shapes and sizes, from the very traditional, religious, and spiritual, to those that are simple, casual, and fun. There are many things to consider when you are planning a celebration with your daughter, such as family traditions, current values, her relationships with her friends and other family and community members, and most importantly, her unique self. Would your daughter be more comfortable with a festive, lively party or with an intimate and quiet ceremony? What kind of ceremony would you like her to have? Are these two answers the same?

Ceremonial altars, readings, and rituals are what distinguish a coming-of-age celebration from an ordinary birthday party and can therefore lend more meaning to your event. Would you like to include prayers or blessings? Though not all ceremonies have altars, an altar can be a center point around which the ritual or ceremony revolves. The altar may be a collective creation put together from the gifts and offerings given to your daughter by her guests, or it can be one that the two of you create together to reflect her rite of passage. Symbols are used as metaphors, the language of ritual, and are usually placed upon the altar. For example, a well-loved bear or doll on the altar might symbolize the childhood she is leaving, and a bouquet of pink rosebuds might symbolize the woman she is becoming. A collage of photographs and pictures, artwork from her preschool days, and her baby book might be some of the things you place on the altar. Symbols and altars reflect the intention and significance of your ceremony.

When and where would you like to have the ceremony? Two essential considerations in planning a ritual are what Kathleen Wall, co-author of *Rites of Passage—Celebrating Life's Changes*, calls "exclusive time" and "exclusive space." "Exclusive time" means that the designated time for the ritual is a priority and ensures that there will be no interruptions. It might also mean that the chosen date has a special significance.

When would you and your daughter like the celebration to be? Would you like to hold it on or near her birthday? Or is there another time of year that has special significance to you or your family? Maybe a solstice or equinox? Spring, the time of the maiden? Or during your religious holy days? Would you like it to be at the time of the full or new moon, or during a significant planetary alignment? Also, is there a time of day (morning, afternoon, or evening) that you prefer?

This celebration marks an important moment in the passage of time, and the timing is important.

"Exclusive space" implies a special setting, an out-of-the-ordinary location. Traditional rites of passage have often included leaving home or taking some kind of journey. Where would you like your celebration to be? Is there a place that is special to your daughter or your family? Would you like the ceremony to be indoors or in an outdoor setting? Your own home or the home of someone special to you might feel most comfortable, or, if you are having a large celebration, you may want to rent a hall or room to create a special mood or to have enough space for everyone. The time of day and year may help in determining the location.

If you and your daughter prefer to hold the ceremony in the comfort of your own home, you can transform this ordinary space into an exclusive and sacred place by adding music, flowers, candles, and other festive, seasonal, or symbolic decorations. Do you or any of your friends or family members play a musical instrument? Does your daughter have a favorite song, now or from her younger years? All of these can help to enhance the mood of the celebration.

Who would you and your daughter like to include in her ceremony? Her friends? Your friends? Family members? In deciding this, you might consider the people who have been and currently are the most significant in your lives. Also, who are the people that you both feel most comfortable with? Who do you think really knows your daughter well enough to celebrate this turning point in her life?

No celebration would be complete without food, and food is an essential part of every ritual. What kind of food or refreshments would you like? Does your celebration include brunch, lunch, or dinner? Would you like your guests to bring the food? Would you like to make it yourself or have it catered?

Give yourself enough time to carefully consider and organize the details—the who, what, when, where, and how. Be as clear and specific as possible with your wishes, invitations, and special requests. If you are asking others to contribute, especially something from their heart such as a special symbol, gift, or reading (something many of your guests will want to do), give them time to carefully consider their role in their ceremony. For everyone involved, it would be wise to start planning several months in advance to ensure that the day is easy, relaxed, and enjoyable.

Planning the ceremony together with your daughter will ensure that she has input into and ownership of the occasion, and the key word here is *together*.

COMING OF AGE TOGETHER

As my own daughter Mikaila was nearing age thirteen, I knew that I wanted her to have a coming-of-age ceremony. Fortunately, the concept was not entirely foreign to her. She had already attended several different ceremonies for her friends, and she knew that at some point it would be her turn to be honored.

While thinking about my daughter, I began to remember my own coming-of-age ceremony. At thirteen, I had been confirmed in the Catholic tradition. As a coming-of-age program, the process had all the right parts: a mentor/sponsor, preparation and training, and a ceremony. The intention was a confirmation of faith, but until recently, I didn't understand that it had been my rite of passage. In retrospect, what was missing for me was the chance to contribute to the process in a more personal way. So I wanted it to be different for my daughter.

When I suggested to her that we begin to plan a ceremony for her, she was eager to be involved in the process. Based on what we had already seen, we had examples to choose from, several of which are described in this chapter. She was most clear about how she did not want it to be, and from there we began to design it according to her comfort level. We started by talking about size, and it quickly became apparent that small and low-key would be best for her. Who would attend was also pretty clear, since she has a significant group of friends whose families are part of our homeschool community. It was important to both of us to acknowledge the important women in her life—the mothers of her closest friends—so we decided on a mother–daughter ceremony. Then we considered the format, primarily where and when. Borrowing from an idea I had read about in Mary Pipher's *The Shelter of Each Other*, we decided on a campout, with a ceremony to be held around the evening fire.

We invited our guests well in advance to accommodate their busy, full lives. There were twelve of us all together, six mothers and their daughters. We asked each pair to bring something either for breakfast or dinner, and collectively assembled enough camping gear to get us through one night pretty comfortably. It was not intended to be a wilderness adventure!

We left the rest of our families at home and set off together one Friday afternoon for a local campground on the beach. Being with my oldest daughter without her siblings felt like another way to acknowledge our unique connection and our journey together. Setting up camp was chaotic and fun, as we secured our tents and discovered all the things we had forgotten to pack. After dinner, the daughters giggled and joked with each other as the mothers put together an altar that was to be the center of our ceremony. Though it was a bit windy, we were able to light candles and hold down photographs with rocks. Gifts were added to the altar by each of our guests. In the end, we did manage to create a strong and warming campfire, the backdrop for our simple ceremony. Then, in honor of our request, each mother and daughter presented my daughter with a quilt square embroidered with a memory, wish, or design that they felt captured Mikaila's spirit. We were both overwhelmed by the amount of love that was offered. Listening together through tears and laughter, I could feel us melt into each other as I held her on my lap.

We awoke the next morning to bright sunshine and an ocean breeze and had a camp-style breakfast of pancakes, sausage, coffee, and hot cocoa. The girls then donned colorful fairy outfits with halos and wings and danced and frolicked on the beach. While the other mothers were cleaning up and preparing to break down the campsite, for the first time since we had arrived, I found myself alone.

As I watched Mikaila with her friends, I thought about the years and the experiences that had brought us to this point in time.

There are moments when I remember and miss the toddler who was notorious for diving off the front porch headfirst to get to her stroller, and the one I held through nights of asthma. I remember the hectic mornings of trying to wrestle her into her clothes for preschool, coffee in one hand, car keys abandoned in the middle of the floor, in an attempt to get to work on time. I remember the way she began to put together her own outfits, with her own unique logic justifying why each piece matched. I remember the frustrations, the power struggles, and the moments of self-doubt. I remember wishing she were more self-reliant, and years later wishing she were still as reliant on me as she used to be. I remember her first signs of puberty and my consequent concerns, fears, and self-doubt.

The mothers and daughters that surrounded us at her ceremony weren't just her friends of the moment or the mothers who helped me carpool. They shared our history, affirmed who we are, and offered us a continuing source of love and support. They helped us create the web that had allowed us to grow, change, and stay connected. My daughter and I did not disconnect as I had feared we would. Instead, our connection has become more elastic, allowing us to push and pull against each other. Her world has expanded, and she feels the confidence of knowing herself better and being connected to something larger. At times it is clear that *she* is the wise one.

And together, we will continue our journey.

Bibliography

Many books and resources contributed greatly to our book and offered essential sources of support and inspiration. We are grateful for the insight, wisdom, and knowledge of all of the authors who contributed to our project.

Books

Allen, Paula Gunn. *Grandmothers of the Light—A Medicine Woman's Sourcebook.* Beacon Press, 1991.

Anderson, David A. *What You Can See, You Can Be!* Devorss & Company, 1988.

Ardinger, Barbara, Ph.D. *A Woman's Book of Rituals and Celebrations.* New World Library, 1992.

Arrien, Angeles. *The Nine Muses—A Mythological Path to Creativity.* Tarcher, 2000.

Atwood, Mary Dean. *Spirit Healing: Native American Magic and Medicine.* Sterling Publishing Co., 1991.

Ban Breathnach, Sarah. *Simple Abundance—A Daybook of Comfort and Joy.* Warner Books, 1995.

Barbach, Lonnie Garfield Ph.D. *For Yourself—The Fulfillment of Female Sexuality.* NAL/Dutton, 1991.

Baring, Anne and Andrew Harvey. *The Divine Feminine— Exploring the Feminine Face of God Throughout the World.* Conari Press, 1996.

Bell, Ruth. *Changing Bodies, Changing Lives.* Vintage Books, 1988.

Blackman, Lynne and Kathy Corey. *A Place to Dream.* Warner Treasures, 1997.

Bodine, Echo. *A Still, Small Voice—A Psychic's Guide to Awakening Intuition.* New World Library, 2001.

Bolen, Jean Shinoda. *Goddesses in Everywoman.* Harper, 1984.

Borysenko, Joan Ph.D. *A Woman's Book of Life—The Biology, Psychology, and Spirituality of the Feminine Life Cycle.* Riverhead Books, 1996.

Borysenko, Joan, Ph.D. *A Woman's Journey to God.* Riverhead Books, 1999.

Boylan, Kristi Meisenbach. *The Seven Sacred Rites of Menarche—The Spiritual Journey of the Adolescent Girl.* Santa Monica Press, 2001.

Brumberg, Joan Jacobs. *The Body Project—An Intimate History of American Girls.* Vintage Books, 1997.

Cameron, Anne. *Daughters of Copper Woman.* Harbour Publishing, 2002.

Cameron, Julia. *The Artist's Way: A Spiritual Path to Higher Creativity.* Tarcher/Putnam, 1992.

Catford, Loran Ph.D. and Michael Ray, Ph.D. *The Path of the Everyday Hero.* Tarcher 1991.

Cherry, Lynne. *The Great Kapok Tree.* Trumpet Club, 1990.

Choquette, Sonia. *The Psychic Pathway—A Workbook for Reawakening the Voice of Your Soul.* Three Rivers Press, 1995.

Choquette, Sonia. *The Wise Child—A Spiritual Guide to Nurturing Your Child's Intuition.* Three Rivers Press, 1999.

Cook, Karin. *What Girls Learn.* Vintage Books, 1997.

Dadona, Cynthia. *Diary of a Modern-day Goddess.* Health Communications, 2000.

Debold, Elizabeth, Idelisse Malave and Marie Wilson. *The Mother Daughter Revolution.* Bantam Doubleday, 1994.

Duerk, Judith. *Circle of Stones—Woman's Journey to Herself.* Innisfree Press, 1999.

Duerk, Judith. *I Sit Listening to the Wind—Woman's Encounter Within Herself.* LuraMedia, 1993.

Edelman, Hope. *Motherless Daughters—The Legacy of Loss.* Addison-Wesley, 1994.

Edwards, Betty. *Drawing on the Right Side of the Brain—A Course in Enhancing Creativity and Artistic Confidence.* Tarcher, 1989.

Estes, Clarissa Pinkola Ph.D. *Women Who Run with the Wolves—Myths and Stories of the Wild Woman Archetype.* Ballantine Books, 1992.

Faraday, Ann. *The Dream Game.* AFAR Publishing, 1974.

Garfield, Patricia L. Ph.D. *Creative Dreaming: Plan and Control Your Dreams to Develop Creativity, Overcome Fears, Solve Problems and Create a Better Self.* Fireside, 1975.

Gawain, Shakti. *Creative Visualization.* New World Library, 1995.

Goodman, Ellen and Patricia O'Brien. *I Know Just What You Mean —The Power of Friendship in Women's Lives.* Simon & Schuster, 2000.

Graham, Lanier. *Goddesses in Art.* Artabras, 1997.

Gravelle, Karen and Jennifer Gravelle. *The Period Book—Everything You Don't Want to Ask (But Need to Know).* Walker & Co., 1996.

Hanh, Thich Nhat. *Present Moment, Wonderful Moment—Mindfulness Verses for Daily Living.* Parallax Press, 1990.

Hanh, Thich Nhat. *The Heart of the Buddha's Teaching.* Parallax Press, 1998.

Harding, M. Esther. *Woman's Mysteries—Ancient and Modern.* Pantheon Books, 1955.

Helgesen, Sally. *The Female Advantage—Women's Ways of Leadership.* Doubleday, 1995.

Herron, Elizabeth. *The Fierce Beauty Club—Girlfriends Discovering Power and Celebrating Body and Soul.* Fair Winds Press, 2001.

Johnson, Anne Akers. *The Body Book—Recipes for Natural Body Care.* Klutz, 2000.

Kasl, Charlotte. *If the Buddha Married.* Penguin, 2001.

Louden, Jennifer. *The Comfort Queen's Guide to Life.* Harmony Books, 2000.

Louden, Jennifer. *The Woman's Retreat Book.* HarperSanFrancisco, 1997.

Marriott, Alice and Carol Rachlin. *American Indian Mythology.* Times Mirror, 1968.

Mellick, Jill. *The Art of Dreaming—Tools for Creative Dream Work.* Conari Press, 1996.

Myss, Caroline. *Sacred Contracts—Awakening Your Divine Potential.* Harmony Books, 2001.

Northrup, Christiane, M.D. *Women's Bodies, Women's Wisdom.* Bantam Books, 1994.

Orloff, Judith, M.D. *Dr. Judith Orloff's Guide to Intuitive Healing.* Times Books, 2000.

Oughton, Jerrie. *The Magic Weaver of Rugs: A Tale of the Navajo.* Houghton Mifflin Co, 1994.

Orenstein, Peggy. *Schoolgirls: Young Women, Self-Esteem, and the Confidence Gap.* Anchor, 1995.

Palmer, Pat. *The Mouse, the Monster and Me—Assertiveness for Young People.* Impact Publishers, 1977.

Peck, M. Scott. *The Different Drum—Community Making and Peace.* Touchstone Books, 1998.

Peterson, Jean Sunde. *Talk with Teens about Self and Stress—50 Guided Discussions for School and Counseling Groups.* Free Spirit Publishing, 1990.

Philip, Neil. *The Illustrated Book of Myths, Tales and Legends of the World.* Dorling Kindersley Limited, 1995.

Pipher, Mary Ph.D. *Reviving Ophelia—Saving the Selves of Adolescent Girls.* Ballantine Books, 1994.

Pipher, Mary Ph.D. *The Shelter of Each Other.* Grosset/Putnam, 1996.

Pollock, Penny. *When the Moon Is Full—A Lunar Year.* Little Brown and Company, 2001.

Rattigan, Jama Kim. *The Woman in the Moon—A Story From Hawai'i.* Little Brown and Company, 1996.

Roth, Geneen. *Breaking Free from Compulsive Eating.* Bobbs-Merrill, 1984.

Rutter, Virginia Beane. *Celebrating Girls—Nurturing and Empowering Our Daughters.* Conari Press, 1996.

SARK. *Change Your Life without Getting Out of Bed—The Ultimate Nap Book.* Fireside, 1999.

SARK. *Living Juicy—Daily Morsels for Your Creative Soul.* Celestial Arts, 1994.

Sarriugarte, Tracy and Peggy Rowe Ward. *Making Friends with Time.* PBJ Productions, 1999.

Shinn, Florence Scovel. *The Wisdom of Florence Scovel Shinn.* Simon & Schuster, 1989.

Shulman, Alix Kates. *Drinking the Rain.* Penguin Books, 1995.

Signell, Karen Ph.D. *Wisdom of the Heart: Working with Women's Dreams.* Bantam Doubleday, 1990.

Sjöö, Monica and Barbara Mor. *The Great Cosmic Mother: Rediscovering the Religion of the Earth.* HarperSanFrancisco, 1987.

Spretnak, Charlene. *Lost Goddesses of Early Greece — A Collection of Pre-Hellenic Myths.* Beacon Press, 1978.

Stassinopoulos, Agapi. *Conversations with the Goddesses — Revealing the Divine Power Within You.* Stewart, Tabori & Chang, 1999.

Stone, Sidra. *The Shadow King — The Invisible Force that Holds Women Back.* Nataraj, 1997.

Taylor, Dena. *Red Flower — Rethinking Menstruation.* The Crossing Press, 1988.

The American Girl Library. *The Care & Keeping of You — The Body Book for Girls.* Pleasant Company, 1998.

The American Girl Library. *A Smart Girl's Guide to Boys — Surviving Crushes, Staying True to Yourself & Other Stuff.* Pleasant Company, 2001.

The Boston Women's Health Book Collective. *The New Our Bodies, Our Selves — A Book by and for Women.* 1984.

Ueland, Brenda. *If You Want to Write — A Book About Art, Independence and Spirit.* Gray Wolf Press, 1987.

Waldherr, Kris. *The Book of Goddesses.* Beyond Words, 1995.

Wall, Kathleen Ph.D. and Gary Ferguson. *Rites of Passage — Celebrating Life's Changes.* Beyond Words, 1998.

Willis, Mariaemma and Victoria Kindle Hodson. *Discover Your Child's Learning Style.* Prima Publishing, 1999.

Movies

American Pie. Universal Pictures, 1999.

Fried Green Tomatoes. Universal Pictures, 1991.

How to Make an American Quilt. Universal Pictures, 1995.

Sirens. Miramax Films, 1994.

Stealing Beauty. Fox Searchlight Pictures, 1996.

Steel Magnolias. TriStar Pictures, 1989.

About the Authors

Janet Lucy, M.A. has been a teacher and therapist for over twenty years. She specializes in a unique process she calls *Soul Work—Discover and Celebrate Your True Self*, and works primarily with women and mothers. Janet offers individual consultations, women's weekly writing groups, and workshops to inspire self-discovery and creative expression. She is the mother of two preteen daughters and lives in Santa Barbara, California, with her husband and children.

Terri Allison has been a teacher and educational administrator for over twenty years. She currently works in an alternative homeschooling program with preteens and teens. She is actively involved in coming-of-age programs through the Unitarian Society of Santa Barbara and in her local community. Terri is the mother of two teenage daughters and a preteen son. She lives with her husband and children in Santa Barbara, California.